T0209677

MACAT

An Analysis of

# Thomas Piketty's

## Capital in the Twenty-First Century

Nick Broten

ROUTLEDGE

Published by Macat International Ltd
24:13 Coda Centre, 189 Munster Road, London SW6 6AW.

Distributed exclusively by Routledge
2 Park Square, Milton Park, Abingdon, Oxon OX14 4RN
711 Third Avenue, New York, NY 10017, USA

*Routledge is an imprint of the Taylor & Francis Group, an informa business*

www.macat.com
info@macat.com

*Cataloguing in Publication Data*
A catalogue record for this book is available from the British Library.
Library of Congress Cataloguing-in-Publication Data is available upon request.
Cover illustration: Etienne Gilfillan

ISBN 978-1-912302-30-7 (hardback)
ISBN 978-1-912127-71-9 (paperback)
ISBN 978-1-912281-18-3 (e-book)

**Notice**
The information in this book is designed to orientate readers of the work under analysis,
to elucidate and contextualise its key ideas and themes, and to aid in the development
of critical thinking skills. It is not meant to be used, nor should it be used, as a
substitute for original thinking or in place of original writing or research. References and
notes are provided for informational purposes and their presence does not constitute
endorsement of the information or opinions therein. This book is presented solely for
educational purposes. It is sold on the understanding that the publisher is not engaged
to provide any scholarly advice. The publisher has made every effort to ensure that
this book is accurate and up-to-date, but makes no warranties or representations with
regard to the completeness or reliability of the information it contains. The information
and the opinions provided herein are not guaranteed or warranted to produce particular
results and may not be suitable for students of every ability. The publisher shall not be
liable for any loss, damage or disruption arising from any errors or omissions, or from
the use of this book, including, but not limited to, special, incidental, consequential or
other damages caused, or alleged to have been caused, directly or indirectly, by the
information contained within.

# CONTENTS

# THE MACAT LIBRARY

The Macat Library is a series of unique academic explorations of seminal works in the humanities and social sciences – books and papers that have had a significant and widely recognised impact on their disciplines. It has been created to serve as much more than just a summary of what lies between the covers of a great book. It illuminates and explores the influences on, ideas of, and impact of that book. Our goal is to offer a learning resource that encourages critical thinking and fosters a better, deeper understanding of important ideas.

Each publication is divided into three Sections: Influences, Ideas, and Impact. Each Section has four Modules. These explore every important facet of the work, and the responses to it.

This Section-Module structure makes a Macat Library book easy to use, but it has another important feature. Because each Macat book is written to the same format, it is possible (and encouraged!) to cross-reference multiple Macat books along the same lines of inquiry or research. This allows the reader to open up interesting interdisciplinary pathways.

To further aid your reading, lists of glossary terms and people mentioned are included at the end of this book (these are indicated by an asterisk [*] throughout) – as well as a list of works cited.

Macat has worked with the University of Cambridge to identify the elements of critical thinking and understand the ways in which six different skills combine to enable effective thinking. Three allow us to fully understand a problem; three more give us the tools to solve it. Together, these six skills make up the **PACIER** model of critical thinking. They are:

**ANALYSIS** – understanding how an argument is built
**EVALUATION** – exploring the strengths and weaknesses of an argument
**INTERPRETATION** – understanding issues of meaning

**CREATIVE THINKING** – coming up with new ideas and fresh connections
**PROBLEM-SOLVING** – producing strong solutions
**REASONING** – creating strong arguments

To find out more, visit **WWW.MACAT.COM.**

# CRITICAL THINKING AND
## *CAPITAL IN THE TWENTY-FIRST CENTURY*

### Primary critical thinking skill: EVALUATION
### Secondary critical thinking skill: REASONING

Thomas Piketty is a fine example of an evaluative thinker. In *Capital in the Twenty-First Century*, he not only provides detailed and sustained explanations of why he sees existing arguments relating to income and wealth distribution as flawed, but also gives us very detailed evaluations of the significance of a vast amount of data explaining why incomes is distributed in the ways it is.

As Piketty stresses, "the distribution question... deserves to be studied in a systematic and methodical fashion." This stress on evaluating the significance of data leads him to focus on the central evaluative questions, and look in turn at the acceptability, relevance, and adequacy of existing justifications for the unequal distribution of wealth. In doing so, Piketty applies his understanding of the data to answering the deeply important question of what political structures and what policies are necessary to move us towards a more equal society.

Piketty's evaluation of the data supports his argument that inequality cannot be depended on to reduce over time: indeed, without government intervention, it is highly likely to increase. In addition, he evaluates international data to argue that poor countries do not necessarily become less poor as a result of foreign investment.

This strong emphasis on the interrogation of data, rather than the building mathematical models that are divorced from data, is a defining feature of Piketty's work.

## ABOUT THE AUTHOR OF THE ORIGINAL WORK

Frenchman **Thomas Piketty** is one of the world's leading young economists, whose reputation for challenging established thinking soared with the 2013 publication of *Capital In The Twenty-First Century*. As well as working at the Paris School of Economics, Piketty is currently centennial professor of the newly created International Inequalities Institute at the London School of Economics. In January 2015 he refused his country's Légion d'Honneur award, saying it wasn't down to the French government to decide who is honorable.

## ABOUT THE AUTHOR OF THE ANALYSIS

**Nick Broten** was educated at the California Institute of Technology and the London School of Economics. He is doing postgraduate work at the Pardee RAND Graduate School and works as an assistant policy analyst at RAND. His current policy interests include designing distribution methods for end-of-life care, closing labour market skill gaps, and understanding biases in risk-taking by venture capitalists.

## ABOUT MACAT

### GREAT WORKS FOR CRITICAL THINKING

Macat is focused on making the ideas of the world's great thinkers accessible and comprehensible to everybody, everywhere, in ways that promote the development of enhanced critical thinking skills.

It works with leading academics from the world's top universities to produce new analyses that focus on the ideas and the impact of the most influential works ever written across a wide variety of academic disciplines. Each of the works that sit at the heart of its growing library is an enduring example of great thinking. But by setting them in context – and looking at the influences that shaped their authors, as well as the responses they provoked – Macat encourages readers to look at these classics and game-changers with fresh eyes. Readers learn to think, engage and challenge their ideas, rather than simply accepting them.

'Macat offers an amazing first-of-its-kind tool for interdisciplinary learning and research. Its focus on works that transformed their disciplines and its rigorous approach, drawing on the world's leading experts and educational institutions, opens up a world-class education to anyone.'

**Andreas Schleicher,**
**Director for Education and Skills, Organisation for Economic**
**Co-operation and Development**

'Macat is taking on some of the major challenges in university education ... They have drawn together a strong team of active academics who are producing teaching materials that are novel in the breadth of their approach.'

**Prof Lord Broers,**
**former Vice-Chancellor of the University of Cambridge**

'The Macat vision is exceptionally exciting. It focuses upon new modes of learning which analyse and explain seminal texts which have profoundly influenced world thinking and so social and economic development. It promotes the kind of critical thinking which is essential for any society and economy. This is the learning of the future.'

**Rt Hon Charles Clarke, former UK Secretary of State for Education**

'The Macat analyses provide immediate access to the critical conversation surrounding the books that have shaped their respective discipline, which will make them an invaluable resource to all of those, students and teachers, working in the field.'

**Professor William Tronzo, University of California at San Diego**

# WAYS IN TO THE TEXT

## KEY POINTS

- Thomas Piketty is a French economist who has made major contributions to the study of wealth and income inequality.

- *Capital in the Twenty-First Century* is the result of Piketty spending 15 years gathering real-world data on inequality. This data was sourced from several countries and covers a period of more than two centuries.

- The book makes the argument that market economies do not naturally tend towards equality. In fact, the opposite may be true: that they have a natural tendency towards greater inequality.

### Who Is Thomas Piketty?

Thomas Piketty was born in France in 1971 and is one of the world's leading young economists, best known for his work on wealth* and income* inequality—the gap between the rich and the poor. His academic output since the early 2000s has focused on measuring wealth and income inequality in several countries over the past three centuries. As part of this work, he has built the biggest database on inequality ever assembled.

Piketty was a young academic star in America, receiving a professorship in economics at the Massachusetts Institute of

Technology (MIT) in 1993 when he was just 22. Unhappy with what he considered the over-mathematical American style of economics, however, he stayed there just three years before returning to his hometown of Paris.

In 2006, Piketty played a key role in founding the Paris School of Economics* and, most important for this work, began developing the World Top Incomes Database (WTID).* This huge collection of data forms the backbone of *Capital in the Twenty-First Century* . Since 2001, he has also published several papers on income and wealth inequality, all leading up to the 577-page *Capital*. The book mainly draws on in-depth analyses of the United States, France, Germany, Britain, and Japan and examines the period from the eighteenth to the twenty-first century.

*Capital* is notable for the history and geography it covers, but also for how much attention it received in the news media. Published in 2013 following the financial crisis of 2007–08,* the book appeared at a time when discussions about economic inequality in the United States and Europe were at their peak. Politicians, economists, and the public at large were debating how markets—meaning the economy, which is mostly in private hands—can be regulated to maximize people's welfare and avoid the growing gap between the rich and the poor. This debate is ongoing and, to some extent, Piketty's long-term reputation will depend on how much his forecasts of increasing inequality prove to be true.

## What Does *Capital* Say?

*Capital* challenges the view widely held among economists that the economy has a natural tendency to close the gap between rich and poor. This idea is sometimes associated with the Belarusian–American economist Simon Kuznets* and the Kuznets Curve* that he proposed in the 1950s and 1960s. The Curve is a graph that illustrates Kuznets' finding that, in market economies, inequality will first increase as a country moves from an agricultural to an industrial base, and then it will fall. Kuznets based this idea on the data available to him and saw this pattern emerging in America from the 1870s to the early twentieth century.[1]

In *Capital,* Piketty extends Kuznets' data to the early twenty-first century. He then divides that historical stretch into three periods. The first period—dating from 1871 to the beginning of World War I*— was known as the Belle Epoque* for its peace and artistic flourishing. That period saw very high inequality in Europe and, in a smaller way, the United States. In the period from 1914 to the mid-twentieth century, inequality fell quickly and remained low. Since 1980, inequality has grown in most countries, although the increase has been greatest in the United States. Piketty warns that inequality will heighten further unless governments adopt policies to counter it. He calls for a global tax on wealth.

To Piketty, the three periods he describes in *Capital* confirm his idea that markets will naturally move toward inequality, making the gap between rich and poor bigger, not smaller. Only when major shocks destroyed a sizeable amount of the wealth of the rich did inequality fall to a low level and remain there for some time. These shocks were primarily caused by the following:

- Two World Wars*

- A global depression*—a long term and severe downturn in economic output

- Progressive taxation*—a system whereby higher earners are taxed at a higher rate.

All this leads Piketty in *Capital* to the central conflict of capitalism,* an economic system based on private ownership, private enterprise and the maximization of profit. Throughout history, and with very few exceptions, the rate of return on capital*—the interest or profit you can earn by investing, which he calls $r$ —has been bigger than the growth rate of the economy, which he calls $g$.

Specifically, $r$ has been quite constant—around 5 percent per year—despite big changes to the makeup of capital (for example, the economy going from mostly agricultural to industrial to information-based). Capital means effectively a person's wealth assets, including money, stocks and bonds, and land.

In contrast, for most of human history, $g$ has been close to zero; the total output, including the salaries that most people live off, has not increased. Only in the last two centuries did $g$ reach a level of 1–2 percent. The key point for Piketty is that $r > g$ *(r is greater than g)*. Since capital is mostly held by the rich, even the so-called *rentiers**—people who live off of inherited capital—will be able to grow richer from generation to generation more quickly than people who depend on their work.

*Capital* has already changed the debate about inequality, but the book's long-term impact is yet to be seen. Most leading economists have responded to it in some way, and more generally it has raised the profile of economic research that studies real-world situations. American economist Tyler Cowen* wrote: "Piketty's tome will put capitalist wealth back at the center of public debate, resurrect interest in the subject of wealth distribution, and revolutionize how people view the history of income inequality."[2]

Perhaps most important, Piketty's call for a tax on wealth has entered the political debate. As an example, in his 2015 State of the Union Address,* former US President Barack Obama* attacked gaps in taxes on the wealthy, saying: "Let's close loopholes that lead to inequality by allowing the top 1 percent to avoid paying taxes on their accumulated wealth."[3]

## Why Does *Capital* Matter?

Students reading *Capital* will receive a lesson in the economic history of the two centuries plus that make up the modern industrial period.* The book contains rich historical examples and dozens of charts that visually show the big changes to the economies of several countries over this time. In some cases, notably the United States and France, Piketty explores in-depth the sociological and political factors that shaped how wealth has spread. The huge amounts of data that he has collected allow him to write a rich and detailed account. *Capital* is a good entry point for students with little experience in data analysis, as Piketty's techniques are not complex but still lead to strong conclusions.

*Capital* is also an excellent example of abstract economic reasoning and a good first look at the economy for students without a technical economics background. The book is not just data and charts. Piketty weaves his data together using economic theories in a way that is both simple and yet full of detail. Students who take the time to explore his technical appendix and grasp his main theory will learn how complex situations can be analyzed with simple theoretical tools.[4] In that sense, *Capital* is an excellent introduction to economic modeling, even if some of his ideas are controversial.

More generally, readers of *Capital* will practice their critical-thinking skills. The book's conclusions are clearly stated and well supported with evidence, but big questions surround several of Piketty's ideas. While some readers have criticized the author purely because they don't like the policies he calls for, many others have made strong and thoughtful challenges to *Capital*. Readers who engage with this criticism and decide where they themselves stand will be well equipped to judge other, less thorny, disputes.

## NOTES

1   Simon Kuznets, "Economic Growth and Income Inequality," *The American Economic Review* 45 (1955).

2   Tyler Cowen, "Capital Punishment: Why a Global Tax on Wealth Won't End Inequality," *Foreign Affairs*, December 18, 2014, accessed January 20, 2015, http://www.foreignaffairs.com/articles/141218/tyler-cowen/capital-punishment.

3   Barack Obama, "State of the Union Address," *Medium*, accessed January 20, 2015, https://medium.com/@WhiteHouse/president-obamas-state-of-the-union-address-remarks-as-prepared-for-delivery-55f9825449b2.

4   Thomas Piketty, *Capital in the Twenty-First Century* (Cambridge: Harvard University Press, 2014), "Technical Appendix of the Book," accessed, January 20, 2015,http://piketty.pse.ens.fr/files/capital21c/en/Piketty2014FiguresTablesLinks.pdf.

# SECTION 1
## INFLUENCES

# MODULE 1
# THE AUTHOR AND THE HISTORICAL CONTEXT

## KEY POINTS

- *Capital in the Twenty-First Century* is the most comprehensive analysis of wealth* and income* inequality ever published. It has received a lot of attention, especially since it came out in 2013 at the tail end the 2007–08 financial crisis.

- Thomas Piketty's family background and education exposed him to two intellectual traditions that come through in *Capital*. The political activity of his parents interested him in making the world more just. And his formal training in mathematics and economics taught him to use hard data to address social problems.

- Piketty was 18 when the Berlin Wall* came down. The collapse of the Soviet Union* quickly followed. Both those events made him skeptical of the communist* alternative to capitalism.*

### Why Read this Text?

Thomas Piketty's *Capital in the Twenty-First Century* is a key work in the study of long-term trends in wealth and income inequality—the gap between the rich and the poor. Its main contribution is in mining huge amounts of data collected from several countries from the eighteenth to the early twenty-first centuries. In this way, the book provides a more complete picture of historical trends in inequality than any previous work. By looking at several centuries, Piketty is able to challenge some commonly held beliefs, such as the view that inequality tends to rise as a country begins to develop a modern

> **❝** When he was growing up, [Piketty's] intellectual role models were French historians and philosophers of the left, rather than economists ... Compared with their scholarship, much of the economics that Piketty encountered at M.I.T. seemed arid and pointless. **❞**
>
> John Cassidy, "Forces of Divergence," *The New Yorker*

economy and then gradually falls as the economy grows. The data also provides Piketty with evidence with which to forecast future trends. Some of what he predicts is highly controversial.

The importance of the book is in many ways tied to when it came out. *Capital* was published in 2013, in the wake of the financial crisis that began in 2007–08. Some people used the book as a sort of scholarly guidebook to support their protests against the great gaps in income and wealth in society. The book seemed to support the slogan of the global protest movement Occupy:* "We are the 99 percent." The slogan suggested that those people who make up the richest 1 percent of the population[1] could not justify the gap in wealth between themselves and the rest of society.

Published in that highly politicized climate, *Capital* received a lot of press attention. Many economists responded to its claims, both positively and negatively. As such, *Capital* helped raise the level of academic research on inequality and also stimulated discussions about the issue, both among economists and the wider public. It will take some time, however, for the book's full impact to become clear.

### Author's Life

Piketty was born in 1971 in Clichy, France, a suburb of Paris. His parents were active in left-wing politics, and as a young man, Piketty was influenced less by economists than historians and philosophers— many of whom had been involved in France's revolutionary politics of the 1960s, particularly the demonstrations of May 1968. In that month, students and laborers went on strike throughout the country to protest capitalism and the inequality that accompanied it.[2] Piketty was a gifted and serious student and he earned a Masters degree in mathematics at an elite French university, the Ecole Normale Supérieure, when he was just 19. He then gained a PhD in Economics at the London School of Economics at the remarkably young age of 22.

Piketty got his first academic job in 1993, when he was appointed an assistant professor of economics at the Massachusetts Institute of Technology, one of the most admired economics departments in the world. Yet Piketty soon grew disillusioned with the department. In his book, he writes about his disappointment during that period with the "childish passion for mathematics" among American economists. He describes how he wanted to study how the world *works*, rather than abstract mathematical rules and ideas.[3] Perhaps guided by this unhappiness with American economists, Piketty returned to Paris in 1995 and began his study of income inequality at the French National Centre for Scientific Research,* the country's largest research institution.

Since returning to France, Piketty has been deeply involved in both academic and political life. In 2002, the country's leading newspaper, *Le Monde*, named him the best young economist in France, and in 2006 he helped set up the Paris School of Economics,* where he has remained as a professor.[4] The institution was important for him as he researched and wrote *Capital* because it maintains the "World Top Incomes Database (WTID)."* Throughout the book, Piketty discusses the information contained in this database.

## Author's Background

The details of Piketty's biography shed some light on the positions he takes on current issues. The son of social activists, he naturally supports what he calls a "just social order."[5] In the introduction to the book, he points to the *Declaration of the Rights of Man and the Citizen*,* a key human-rights statement written in 1789 at the start of the French Revolution.* Article I of the *Declaration* states: "Men are born and remain free and equal in rights. Social distinctions may be founded only on the general good."[6]

This notion—that some people should have a more privileged place in society *only* if that helps the population as a whole—is a kind of moral standard for *Capital in the Twenty-First Century*. Through the length of his work, Piketty looks at whether the social differences between rich and poor in a capitalist system respect this standard. Piketty turned 18 in 1989. He says the fact that his passage into adulthood happened to fall on the 200th anniversary of the *Declaration* certainly played a role in the development of his ideas.[7]

Another important event in 1989 was the fall of the Berlin Wall, a key symbol of the barrier between communist East and capitalist West. Its demolition—signaling the end of the communist system in East Germany and the Soviet Union that had sought to eliminate inequality through collective ownership—seems to have dampened any of the more revolutionary feelings the author might have had. Having witnessed the failure of the communist experiment in equality in the Soviet Union, he was "vaccinated for life against the conventional but lazy rhetoric of anti-capitalism." That way of thinking, he believed, "ignored the historic failure of communism" and "turned its back on the intellectual means necessary to push beyond it."[8]

Those influences, along with his experience of political activism in France, helped shape *Capital*. So too did Piketty's views of the "American Dream:"* the set of ideals associated with the United States that include social mobility, economic security and the chance to live a happy life.[9]

## NOTES

1    "We are the 99 Percent,"
     http://wearethe99percent.tumblr.com/ accessed December 17, 2014.

2    John Cassidy, "Forces of Divergence," *New Yorker*, March 31, 2014,
     accessed December 1, 2014,
     http://www.newyorker.com/magazine/2014/03/31/forces-of-divergence.

3    Thomas Piketty, *Capital in the Twenty-First Century* (Cambridge: Harvard
     University Press, 2014), 32.

4    Paris School of Economics, "Thomas Piketty Curriculum Vitae," accessed
     December 1, 2014,
     http://piketty.pse.ens.fr/fr/cv-fr.

5    Piketty, *Capital*, 31.

6    "Yale Law School, the Avalon Project, "Declaration of the Rights of Man,"
     accessed December 17, 2014,
     http://avalon.law.yale.edu/18th_century/rightsof.asp.

7    Piketty, *Capital*, 479.

8    Piketty, *Capital*, 31.

9    Piketty, *Capital*, 31.

# ACADEMIC CONTEXT

## KEY POINTS

- Economics is concerned with the production and distribution of goods in society and with aspects of human behavior. Thomas Piketty's primary field of public economics deals with the relationship between government policy and general welfare.

- Most of the classical economists* who inspired Piketty based their work on specific social concerns, such as the wealth gap between rich and poor or industrial policies.

- *Capital in the Twenty-First Century* is part of the modern "empirical" tradition of economics, which is based on collecting and analyzing data. The tradition began with Simon Kuznets's* work to create a national accounting system to measure such things as Gross Domestic Product*—the market value of all goods and services within a country's borders at a given time.

### The Work In Its Context

According to British economist Lionel Robbins's* famous definition of 1932, "Economics is the science which studies human behavior as a relationship between given ends and scarce means which have alternative uses."[1] Three things about this definition stand out.

First, the idea that economics is a science is key for understanding how it is practiced in the real world. Economists have always tried to make contributions to government policy. Most of the famous works of economics have been useful both as academic research and in helping to set policy. The key text of modern economics, Adam Smith's* *Wealth of Nations* (1776), presented a theoretical model for

> ❝ Piketty's worry about the rich getting richer is indeed merely 'the latest' of a long series going back to Malthus and Ricardo and Marx. ❞
>
> Deirdre McCloskey, in her review of *Capital in the Twenty-First Century*

how markets work. It also challenged Britain's mercantilist* policies of the time, which primarily blocked free trade.

Yet some economists believe that economic theory is basically something separate from the real world. Ariel Rubinstein,* a noted Israeli economist, has compared economic models to "fables" or "fairy tales." He suggests that such economic models are more like stories than concrete descriptions of real life.[2]

Second, economics deals with scarce*—that is, limited—resources, so it has always been concerned with how those resources are distributed in society. Certain goods are in plentiful supply. For example, there is plenty of air and it is more or less equally distributed to everyone. But many other goods—for example fast cars and medicines—are almost always not equally distributed. Much of economics is focused on understanding how resources and goods can be distributed most efficiently—in other words, how to make improvements in the distribution of income and wealth so that everyone comes out better.

Finally, economics is concerned with certain elements of human behavior. Economic research usually does not deal directly with love or hate, but it does focus on what motivates people to participate in economic activity. Generally speaking, economists assume people try to get the most they can. They prefer more to less, and better to worse.[3]

## Overview of the Field

In some ways, *Capital in the Twenty-First Century* is part of the classical* tradition in economics, the first school of modern economic thought associated with thinkers like Thomas Malthus,* Adam Smith, David Ricardo,* and Karl Marx.* Each of those economists were motivated by specific concerns about society.[4] Of them, Ricardo and Marx are most important for understanding *Capital.*

The British political economist David Ricardo lived two centuries ago. One of his main concerns was the overall threat to society from land becoming more and more expensive. He recognized that land was a scarce resource—there is a given quantity of land and you can't make more of it.

That fact was particularly important in Ricardo's time, when most people were small farmers. Ricardo observed that as population increased, more people would be bidding for a piece of land, thereby driving up its price. That would increase the wealth and economic power of landowners who lived off the money they made by renting out their land.[5] If that trend continued, the economy would become so concentrated in the hands of landowners that society would become unbalanced.

To make his argument, Ricardo developed the "scarcity principle." If something is scarce and demand for it is high—as was land in the example, or as diamonds are today—its price will rise until demand for it falls to the level where it equals supply. At that price, supply and demand are said to be at an equilibrium level.*[6] This remains an important element of the theory of supply and demand* used in economics today.

Writing roughly 50 years after Ricardo, the German philosopher and economist Karl Marx was less concerned with rising land rents than with the rise of industrial capitalism.* Marx adapted Ricardo's scarcity principle, and developed a theory of "infinite accumulation," or the "inexorable [unstoppable] tendency for capital to be concentrated in ever fewer hands, with no limit."[7]

The logic of Marx's analysis is similar to Ricardo's. As society develops, people demand more goods. Capitalists—business owners and investors—respond by producing more. The profits they earn allow them to amass more capital: money or other items that can be invested to produce more goods. This cycle will then continue until either the value of capital drops or capital becomes so concentrated in a few hands that society falls apart. These sometimes controversial economic theories are not new. But they remain important notions, used by some economists in their research in the field today.

Among current economists, Piketty is associated with the field of public economics. Broadly speaking, public economics is concerned with the links between government policy and "economic welfare"—or how well off people are. Some of the specific areas that public economists study include what the best tax policies might be, how efficient government programs are, and the causes of—and solutions to—market failures. A recent, serious example of such a failure was the collapse of the housing market that set off the global financial crisis of 2007–08.*

### Academic Influences

*Capital* is also part of an important—though somewhat dry—tradition of economics based on collecting and analyzing data. That tradition begins with the work of the twentieth century Belarusian-American economist Simon Kuznets. After the Great Depression* of the 1930s that started in the United States and resulted in a global economic crisis, Kuznets supervised a program to develop ways to measure the American economy—including metrics that became known as the Gross Domestic Product* and the Gross National Product.* Prior to that time, no such tools existed. When US President Herbert Hoover* tried to counter the Depression, he did so using only "sketchy data such as stock price indices, freight car loadings, and incomplete indices of industrial production."[8] The accounting tools that Kuznets developed have since become central to economic policy-making.

Kuznets's work allowed him to undertake the first major study of income inequality—the gap in earnings and wealth between the rich and the other layers of society. In 1955, he delivered a lecture to the American Economic Association titled "Economic Growth and Income Inequality," which was then published as a paper. Kuznets himself was careful in describing his findings. He said that the paper contained "5 percent empirical [data-based] information and 95 percent speculation."[9]

Be that as it may, the idea that Kuznets developed was that inequality first increases as a country develops, a period when investors earn high returns while wages tend to be low. But after a number of years, as the economy becomes more mature, inequality falls as wages rise compared to what investors can earn—a process is commonly known as the Kuznets Curve.* When it is put on a graph, the line it forms is called a bell curve, or an inverted U shape. Elementary economics courses often teach this concept, sometimes without Kuznets' warnings about the lack of proof for this idea.

Piketty's research grows directly from Kuznets's work. He himself states that one of his motivations for writing *Capital* was to put Kuznets' findings into a "wider perspective"—to extend them both over time, and beyond the US borders.[10]

## NOTES

1   Lionel Robbins, *An Essay on the Nature and Significance of Economic Science* (London: Macmillan, 1932), 15.

2   Ariel Rubinstein, "Dilemmas of an Economic Theorist," *Econometrica* 74 (2006): 881.

3   Colin Camerer and Ernst Fehr, "When Does 'Economic Man' Dominate Social Behavior?" *Science* 311, no. 5757 (2006) 47–52.

4   Deirdre McCloskey, "Measured, unmeasured, mismeasured, and unjustified pessimism: a review essay of Thomas Piketty's *Capital in the Twenty-First Century*," *Erasmus* 7, no.2 (2014) 5.

5   McCloskey, "Measured, unmeasured, mismeasured," 5.

6    David Ricardo, *Principles of Political Economy and Taxation* (London: Chiswick Press, 1891), 6.

7    Thomas Piketty, *Capital in the Twenty-First Century* (Cambridge: Harvard University Press, 2014), 9.

8    Bureau of Economic Analysis, "GDP: One of the Great Inventions of the 20th Century," accessed December 17, 2014, https://www.bea.gov/scb/account_articles/general/0100od/maintext.htm.

9    Simon Kuznets, "Economic Growth and Income Inequality," *The American Economic Review* (1955), 26.

10   Piketty, *Capital*, 16.

# MODULE 3
# THE PROBLEM

## KEY POINTS

- At the time *Capital in the Twenty-First Century* was published, economists were thinking about why most of them had not been able to predict—and maybe prevent—the financial crisis of 2007–08.* In particular, economists came to feel that many of the mathematical theories widely accepted before the crisis did not realistically describe the world.

- The key debate at the time was between economists in the Keynesian* tradition who saw the crisis as a short-term shock that government spending could help fix, and pro-market economists, who viewed it as evidence of basic weaknesses in the economy.

- Thomas Piketty's work was somewhat separate from this debate, as his ideas were in development well before the crisis. Nonetheless, the shift away from abstract theories made the discipline more receptive to his data-driven work.

### Core Question

In the aftermath of the financial crisis that began in 2007–08, economists were mainly concerned with how to cope with such disasters in the future. They were also unhappily trying to understand why most economists had not seen the crisis coming.

Before the crash, many economists believed in market efficiency. The "efficient–markets hypothesis" (EMH)* developed by Eugene Fama* in the 1970s, for example, summed up their ideas. It states that markets efficiently process information. In other words, buyers and sellers are all aware of news that could affect the value of their assets,

> **❝** The Great Credit Crisis has cast into doubt much of what we thought we knew about economics. We thought that monetary policy had tamed the business cycle ... We thought that financial institutions and markets had come to be self-regulating—that investors could be left largely if not wholly to their own devices. Above all we thought that we had learned how to prevent the kind of financial calamity that struck the world in 1929. We now know that much of what we thought was true was not. **❞**
>
> in *Group Selection* Barry Eichengreen, "The Last Temptation of Risk," *The National Interest*

things that can be bought and sold. So, according to the EMH, prices in financial markets will reflect the real value of stocks, bonds, and other assets.[1] Markets, if left alone, will "clear"—they will find the right prices at which supply equals demand. Everything offered for sale will find a buyer if the price comes down low enough, and (almost) anything you want to buy will be put up for sale if the price is high enough.

EMH takes several forms. The weak version says this holds true only in the long-run. The strong version says that everyday prices always reflect all information in the market, so assets will always have their true price. Aside from rare cases of fraud, no one can sell goods for much above their value, nor carelessly offer them way below their value.

Another related idea that was popular before the crisis was the "real business cycle theory" (RBC theory).* It says that so-called business cycle* fluctuations—a strong economy one year, and a weak one the next—do not mean that the economy is basically unstable. Instead, they are due to "real" causes,[2] such as a sharp rise in oil prices or the introduction of a new technology.

In some ways, RBC theory is similar to the EMH: one deals with financial markets, the other with the economy as a whole. RBC theory had an important message for policy makers. Since fluctuations in the economy are seen as normal responses to outside changes, government interventions in the economy, such as fiscal stimulus*— extra government spending to spur on the economy—will do more harm than good. In broader terms, those theories generally led to the conclusion that if governments left the economy alone, it would automatically produce the best outcome for society.

The recent crisis called those views into question and created an opportunity for the economics discipline to re-evaluate accepted theories. Keynesian economics has come back out on top. This is based on the idea that the economic recessions that hit every few years are typically not due to "real" events like a sharp hike in oil prices. Instead, irrational behavior by investors and wrong government decisions[3] cause them.

John Maynard Keynes,* writing just after the Great Depression of the 1930s,* described the emotions and mistakes that lead to these shocks—or economic slowdowns—as "animal spirits."[4] Importantly, the Keynesian view argues that short-term shocks are not caused by real factors. So fiscal stimulus to boost the economy—government spending to build roads, hire extra teachers, and the like—*can* help bring the economy back to its full potential in the short term.

## The Participants

Several voices, not one or two key books, dominated economic thinking after the recent financial crisis. This also saw several areas of economics that had previously been ignored gained new attention.

Nobel Prize winner Paul Krugman,* one of the most respected Keynesian voices, strongly criticized the widespread support among economists for the "market efficiency" approach in the period leading up to the crisis. Robert Lucas,* another Nobel Prize winner in economics, had trumpeted that approach. In 2003, Lucas wrote that the "central problem of depression prevention has been solved."[5] Inspired by the RBC theory, Lucas and many others believed that serious economic shocks—or recessions—were a thing of the past.

To Krugman, such optimism— and the style of economics supporting it—was misguided. He wrote: "Economics went astray because economists, as a group, mistook beauty, clad in impressive-looking mathematics, for truth."[6] By focusing on models that seemed to explain how markets *could* be very efficient, economists "turned a blind eye to the limitations of human rationality that often lead to bubbles and busts."[7] Rather than focus on studying a "perfect, frictionless market system," Krugman believed economists should try better to include the real world in their models.[8]

Not all experts accepted Krugman's diagnosis of the problems within economics and his practical solutions for the economy. Indian economist Raghuram Rajan* viewed the crisis as a symptom of more basic problems: poor education, overly high wages, and other weaknesses. To Rajan, the most important problem was that "advanced economies were losing their ability to grow by making useful things."[9] Rather than inject government money into the economy, Rajan suggested "educating or retraining workers who are falling behind, encouraging entrepreneurship and innovation, and harnessing the power of the financial sector to do good while preventing it from going off track."[10]

As experts thought about what had caused the financial crisis, they began paying more attention to some areas of economics that had been neglected. Economic historians who had studied previous financial crises, such as Barry Eichengreen* and Ben Bernanke* (who was chairman of the US Federal Reserve—America's central bank—in 2007–08), played a bigger role in the public discussions. Behavioral economists, such as Richard Thaler* and Daniel Kahneman,* whose work focused on errors in human judgment, also stood out.

Meanwhile, new organizations, such as the Institute for New Economic Thinking,* emerged to support new types of economic research. Perhaps most important, research based on real-world data got more attention. As Eichengreen writes: "The late-twentieth century was the heyday of deductive economics [based on reasoning] …In contrast, the twenty-first century will be the age of inductive economics [based on observation], when empiricists [who study data collected from the real world] hold sway and advice is grounded in concrete observation of markets and their inhabitants."[11]

## The Contemporary Debate

To some extent, Thomas Piketty was outside of this debate. Piketty and his colleagues began collecting the data for *Capital in the Twenty-First Century* well before the crisis, and these economic debates did not influence his main conclusions in the book. Piketty does discuss the potential link between inequality and the financial crisis in *Capital*, but the debate between Keynesians and pro-market economists—which was going strong in the United States and Britain—had little bearing on the text.

The shifting tone in economics from theory to working with real-world data did, however, influence how people perceived the book. *Capital* is an example of what Eichengreen calls "inductive" economics,* and it is reasonable to think *Capital* would not have reached the audience it did had it been published a decade earlier. Also, the basic idea of the book—that markets may lead to socially undesirable outcomes, such as extreme inequality—was in tune with the post-crisis climate, particularly in the United States and Britain. It is interesting to note that the book was less well received in Piketty's native France, in part because "questions about inequality … have long been central to the political debate there."[12]

As the *Economist* notes: "Drawing attention to resurgent inequality has a sense of novelty in America, but in France it is a political given."[13] The crisis—particularly in the United States, but also in Britain—brought new questions such as how inequality evolves over time to the center of public debate, and Piketty's book was seen to provide some answers.

## NOTES

1  Eugene Fama, "Efficient Capital Markets: A Review of Theory and Empirical Work," *The Journal of Finance* 25 (1970), 383–417.

2  John Long and Charles Plosser, "Real Business Cycles," *Journal of Political Economy* 91 (1983), 39–69.

3  Sarwat Jahan, Ahmed Saber Mahmud, and Chris Papageorgiou, "What is Keynesian Economics?" *Finance and Development,* International Monetary Fund, September 2014, accessed January 20. 2015, http://www.imf.org/external/pubs/ft/fandd/2014/09/basics.htm.

4  John Maynard Keynes, *The General Theory of Employment, Interest and Money* (London: Macmillan, 1936), 161–162.

5  Robert Lucas, "Macroeconomic Priorities," *American Economic Review* (2003), 1.

6  Paul Krugman, "How Did Economists Get It So Wrong?" *The New York Times*, September 6, 2009, accessed January 20 2015, http://www.nytimes.com/2009/09/06/magazine/06Economic-t. html?pagewanted=all.

7  Krugman, "Economists."

8  Krugman, "Economists."

9  Raghuram Rajan, "The True Lessons of the Financial Crisis," *Foreign Affairs*, May/June 2014, accessed December 17, 2014, http://www.foreignaffairs.com/articles/134863/raghuram-g-rajan/the-true-lessons-of-the-recession.

10  Rajan, "True Lessons."

11  Barry Eichengreen, "The Last Temptation of Risk," *The National Interest*, May/June 2009, http://nationalinterest.org/article/the-last-temptation-of-risk-3091, last accessed December 17, 2014.

12 "Le French Touch," *The Economist*, April 28, 2014, accessed February 4, 2015, http://www.economist.com/blogs/charlemagne/2014/04/thomas-piketty.

13 "Le French Touch."

# THE AUTHOR'S CONTRIBUTION

## KEY POINTS

- In order to track income and wealth inequality for several countries for more than two centuries, Piketty and his collaborators collected an enormous amount of data based on tax returns.

- Piketty's data expands the work of economist Simon Kuznets* before him. His aim is to tell the grand story of how and why wealth and income inequality evolves over time. He uses two sets of data: income taxes and estate taxes.

- While many economists study how markets function, Piketty has forged a new specialty in income and wealth inequality that falls between existing academic disciplines.

### Author's Aims

Thomas Piketty's *Capital in the Twenty-First Century* is an example of economics based on observation—rather than work with strictly theoretical models like the efficient markets hypothesis (EMH).* Piketty bases nearly all of his claims in the book on what he observes in the data he has collected. His analysis is rooted in one broad question: "What public policies and institutions bring us closer to an ideal society?"[1]

In this context, *Capital* serves two aims. First, it shows how economics can function as a data-driven discipline exploring historical trends—looking at issues over a couple of centuries. Second, the book also attempts to answer the above question by identifying which political, cultural, and economic arrangements are connected with increasing inequality, and which are connected with decreasing inequality.

> ❝ I quickly realized there had been no significant effort to collect historical data on the dynamics of inequality since Kuznets, yet the profession continued to churn out purely theoretical results without even knowing what facts needed to be explained ... When I returned to France, I set out to collect the missing data.. ❞
>
> Thomas Piketty, *Capital in the Twenty-First Century*

Piketty was not the first to study inequality—the gap between the rich and the other layers of society. Kuznets explored the issue several decades earlier. However, what sets Piketty's analysis apart is its broad historical and geographic view. By gathering an enormously rich collection of data on income and wealth for several countries over more than two centuries, Piketty set out to tell a grand story about inequality—and to create a complete theory of how and why inequality changes over time.

In this way, Piketty's work is different from most economics literature. Theoretical economists typically create unifying theories, but when tested against real-world data, the theories rarely hold up. Most data-based studies, in contrast, cover a much more limited time period and geographical area, and so they rarely offer a broad understanding of the issues.

### Approach

All of Piketty's economic and historical analysis in *Capital* is based on two extensive sets of data. The first is the World Top Incomes Database (WTID),* an ever-growing collection of income statistics for dozens of countries over hundreds of years.[2] Piketty states that his data set "broadens the spatial and temporal limits of Kuznets's innovative and pioneering work," for many countries covering the eighteenth to the twenty-first centuries.[3]

Piketty and his colleagues, including Emmanuel Saez,* Anthony Atkinson,* and Nancy Qian, used tax data to estimate the top income brackets—the top 10 percent, top 1 percent, and even smaller slices of the population—for the United States, Britain, France, Sweden, and Japan. They had data for other countries too, although it was less reliable. The data focuses on the income in the upper income brackets for a practical reason. In most countries before the mid-twentieth century, only people in the upper income brackets paid income taxes.[4]

In addition to covering more countries and many more years, Piketty's work adds other innovations to Kuznets's work. Perhaps most important, Piketty is able to examine much finer fractions of income than Kuznets could. Kuznets focused on the income bracket for the top 1 percent in the United States, but Piketty creates brackets for the top 0.1 and top 0.01 percent, which gives him greater insight into the growing importance of the super-rich.[5]

Piketty's second important source of data tracks not how much people earn, but how much wealth they own. This data is based on estate tax returns—the information that must be provided when someone dies and their wealth is passed on to their heirs. The economist Robert Lampman* pioneered the use of estate tax returns to study wealth inequality—the gap in wealth between the rich and others—in 1962 for the United States, and Atkinson and Alan Harrison[6] later applied that approach to Britain. Alongside Jean-Laurent Rosenthal and Gilles Postel-Vinay, Piketty collected the data for France, which has more extensive information than any of the other countries, dating back to 1807.[7] This wealth data allows Piketty to examine the link between wealth and income, which is central to his argument. The data also enables him to explore the effect of wealth-destroying shocks, like war or financial crises, on inequality.[8]

Piketty's analysis is based on the data he has collected. But he uses a set of theories, and three general laws, to reach his conclusions. These three laws deal with capital,* income,* savings,* and growth.*

## Contribution In Context

Economics has a tradition of critically examining the workings of markets dating back to Karl Marx.* But the study of income and wealth inequality as practiced by Piketty was not a very active area before he and his colleagues began their work. Piketty says this is because inequality "falls into a sort of economic no man's land, too historical for economists and too economistic for historians."[9] In other words this kind of research, which falls between different academic disciplines and takes time to complete, presents a challenge for universities and remains a low priority.

Still, *Capital* builds on a tradition of work based on real-world observations—some written by Piketty himself—that improved the methods to use tax data to determine wealth and income inequality. Kuznets pioneered the effort in the mid-1950s, but major work has taken place between then and now. Typically, tax data provides, for each income bracket (or level), "the corresponding number of taxpayers, as well as their total income and tax liability."[10]

As Atkinson, Saez, and Piketty note, this kind of data presents several challenges. One of the key problems is that you cannot easily use the tax data to calculate, say, the top 1 percent of earners. For example, in Britain in 1911–12, less than 12,000 taxpayers, or roughly 0.05 percent of the population, earned enough to be subject to the top tax rate.[11] To translate that into a percentage such as the top 1 percent of earners, the authors use an estimating technique called interpolation.* While other economists use this technique, Piketty and his colleagues Atkinson and Saez made significant progress on it and other methods related to measuring income inequality.

# NOTES

1   Thomas Piketty, *Capital in the Twenty-First Century* (Cambridge: Harvard University Press, 2014), 574.

2   "Paris School of Economics, World Top Incomes Database," accessed December 22, 2014, http://topincomes.parisschoolofeconomics.eu/.

3   Piketty, *Capital*, 16.

4   Thomas Piketty and Emmanuel Saez, "Income Inequality in the United States, 1913–1998," *Quarterly Journal of Economics* 118 (2003), 4.

5   Piketty and Saez, "Income Inequality."

6   Robert Lampman, "The Share of Top Wealth-Holders in National Wealth, 1922–56," *NBER Books* (1962).

7   Thomas Piketty, "Wealth Concentration in a Developing Economy: Paris and France, 1807–1994," *The American Economic Review* 96 (2006): 236–256.

8   Piketty, *Capital*, 18.

9   Piketty, *Capital*, 17.

10  Anthony Atkinson, Thomas Piketty, and Emmanuel Saez, "Top Incomes in the Long Run of History," *Journal of Economic Literature* 49, no. 1 (2011): 12.

11  Atkinson, Piketty, and Saez, "Top Incomes," 12.

# SECTION 2
## IDEAS

# MODULE 5
# MAIN IDEAS

## KEY POINTS

- Piketty argues that a key driver of inequality is the difference between the rate of return on invested capital and the growth rate of the economy.

- Whereas the economist Simon Kuznets's* traditional view suggested inequality would eventually decrease as countries develop, Piketty's data shows this is not always the case. In fact, inequality may rise indefinitely without targeted policies to reduce the wealth holdings of the very rich.

- *Capital* is written in a readable, accessible style, and is targeted towards both economists and non-economists. The book uses limited jargon and makes an effort to define technical language.

### Key Themes

Thomas Piketty's approach in *Capital in the Twenty-First Century* is based far more on observation than on theory. He sometimes introduces simple economic theory, but his main focus is exploring the evolution of four key things: capital*, income,* the rate of return on capital, and the growth* rate of the economy.[1]

Piketty pays little attention to historical changes in living standards. He is almost exclusively concerned with how the difference in living standards between the rich and other people changes over time. For example, he does not attempt to compare the living standards of the nineteenth century poor with those of the twenty-first century poor. Rather he looks at the position of the poor compared to the rich in each of the periods he studies. In other words, the book focuses on the

> ❝ The process by which wealth is accumulated and distributed contains powerful forces pushing toward divergence, or at any rate toward an extremely high level of inequality. Forces of convergence also exist … but the forces of divergence can at any point regain the upper hand. ❞
>
> Thomas Piketty, *Capital in the Twenty-First Century*

share—or portion—of income and wealth that each layer of society gets.[2] Piketty makes statements such as, "The top decile's [10th's] share of total wealth [in the United States] dropped from 80 to 70 percent," meaning the percentage of the entire economy held by the most wealthy 10 percent of the population fell by 10 percent.[3]

Piketty uses a number of key measures to track the economy over the long term. Most important is capital, which he uses to mean the same as wealth. To Piketty, capital means "all forms of wealth that individuals (or groups of individuals) can own and that can be transferred or traded through the market."[4] Capital includes land, real estate, stocks and bonds, machinery, agricultural commodities, and other assets for which there are functioning markets. Due to the requirement that capital must be something that can be bought or sold, Piketty does not include human capital, such as a person's education and skills, in his analysis of capital.

The other key measure in the book is income, which Piketty measures both for individuals and for countries. For most individuals, income is wages and possibly dividends (a share of the profits of a company in which they own stocks) or interest payments from capital they own. National income is then defined as "the sum of all income available to the residents of a given country in a given year, regardless of the legal classification of that income."[5]

Much of the analysis in the book involves the capital-income ratio,* which Piketty labels $\beta$ (the Greek letter beta). It is calculated by dividing a country's total amount of capital by the total national income in a given year.[6] For example, if a country's capital is worth 100 units, and national income in a given year is 20 units, $\beta$ for that year will be 5—meaning it will take five years of income to accumulate the total capital for that economy.

Piketty claims that $\beta$ is closely linked to inequality. A high $\beta$, meaning low income compared to a country's capital, represents an economy with a low rate of economic growth (since lower income means lower growth) and high savings rates (since a large amount of capital has been saved up). Over time, that will lead to more inequality, as capital continues growing faster than income. If economic growth increases and the rate of savings does not change, $\beta$ will tend to fall, bringing inequality down.[7] This is a key point: simplifying somewhat, Piketty describes inequality—the gap between rich and poor—as higher during periods of stronger capital accumulation* (the growth of a country's wealth), and lower during periods of stronger economic growth.

### Exploring The Ideas

In *Capital*, Piketty pushes against what he calls "economic determinism,"* or the belief that there are natural forces within capitalism* that keep it moving towards greater equality.[8] In fact, Piketty states that "there is no natural, spontaneous process" making society more equal.[9] As a result, he argues that without government action, there is no reason to expect inequality will not rise to very high levels in the future.

The key historical fact in the book is that wealth inequality in Europe and the United States over the last three centuries can be roughly divided into three stages, though each country's experience is somewhat distinct. From the eighteenth century to what was known as the Belle Epoque* at the end of the nineteenth century, private wealth held by the rich was far greater than national income. This means that β was very large—in some places greater than 7.[10] Then, in the aftermath of World War I,* the capital stock—or private and public wealth—shrank rapidly, and β remained low for several decades. In Britain in the 1940s, for example, it was as low as 2.[11] Since the 1970s, inequality has risen nearly everywhere, a trend Piketty expects will continue.

Piketty's explanation for these trends is based on three "fundamental laws of capitalism." The first two are somewhat technical.[12] The third, what he calls the "fundamental force for divergence,"[13] is key. For the vast majority of human history, and in particular since capitalism took off in the eighteenth century, the rate of return on capital, represented by *r*, has been greater than the growth rate of the economy, represented by *g*. The rate of return refers to the average yearly profit or interest you get when you invest your wealth instead of keeping it hidden under your mattress.

The rate of return on capital has been remarkably constant—around 5 percent per year—throughout recorded history, even as the economy has evolved from agricultural to industrial to service-oriented.[14] In contrast, annual growth rates for most of human history were tiny and only reached levels of 1 to 2 percent—and occasionally 3 percent—in the last two centuries.[15]

To Piketty, the fact that the average rate of return is bigger than the average growth rate is what drives the economy towards inequality. When the return on capital exceeds the growth rate (which can be expressed as $r > g$, or *r* is greater than *g*), "it logically follows that inherited wealth grows faster than output and income."[16] Since fewer people than those who earn wage income hold capital, society will tend towards inequality.[17]

As an example, consider two people, Jane and Joe. Both have the same job and earn $100,000 per year. Unlike Joe, Jane has an inheritance of $10 million, which she invests in the stock market, earning a return of 5 percent. Joe has no savings. Assuming both Jane and Joe spend $100,000 per year, let's look at how their total wealth changes over time. After one year, Joe will have made his $100,000, which he immediately spends. Jane will have made $600,000 ($500,000—which is 5 percent of her $10 million capital—and $100,000 from her job). She also spends $100,000 but reinvests the $500,000. After 10 years, Joe's total wealth will have grown very little—perhaps a bit if he can negotiate a raise—while Jane's $10 million will be now be worth more than $16 million. In the beginning of this example, Jane was already much richer than Joe, but by the dynamics of $r > g$, their total wealth is even more unequal at the end.

## Language And Expression

Piketty aimed *Capital* at a broad audience, so the work can be read and understood not only by economists, but also by members of the general public. Piketty rarely uses economic jargon, and when he does he is careful to define his concepts in clear and understandable language. The book is also rich in literary examples, from Jane Austen* to Honoré de Balzac,* and Piketty uses these examples to make his descriptions of real-life situations lively and easy to read.

The character Vautrin from Balzac's novel *Le Père Goriot** appears throughout the book as a fable for the two societies that Piketty describes many times—one in which incomes depend on hard work and one in which income is mostly inherited. As a sign of the society full of inherited money that *Le Père Goriot* describes, Vautrin warns a young law student not to study law but to marry a rich member of the nobility instead. As Piketty writes: "Even if he ranks at the top of his class and quickly achieves a brilliant career in law … he will still have to get by on a mediocre income and give up all hope of becoming truly wealthy."[18] Literary references like this are highly unusual in economics writing and are one of the features that have made *Capital* different.

On the technical side, readers familiar with economics may be confused by the way that Piketty constructs some of his concepts, which are quite unusual. He often refers to the capital–income ratio β, for example, without referring to another widely accepted concept: depreciation* of capital over the long term. In fact, Piketty's data *is* adjusted for depreciation, but he does not always make this clear in the text. Some of the critical comments about the book have mistakenly faulted Piketty for neglecting this idea.

## NOTES

1   Thomas Piketty, *Capital in the Twenty-First Century* (Cambridge: Harvard University Press, 2014), 33.

2   Piketty, *Capital*, 266.

3   Piketty, *Capital*, 349.

4   Piketty, *Capital*, 46.

5   Piketty, *Capital*, 43.

6   Piketty, *Capital*, 50.

7   Piketty, *Capital*, 166.

8   Piketty, *Capital*, 20.

9   Piketty, *Capital*, 21.

10  Piketty, *Capital*, 116.

11  Piketty, *Capital*, 116.

12  Piketty, *Capital*, 52.

13  Piketty, *Capital*, 25.

14  Piketty, *Capital*, 356.

15  Piketty, *Capital*, 356.

16  Piketty, *Capital*, 26.

17  Piketty, *Capital*, 244.

18  Piketty, *Capital*, 239.

# MODULE 6
# SECONDARY IDEAS

## KEY POINTS

- Piketty presents two case studies: France and the United States. Since 1970, while inequality has changed little in France, it has increased sharply in America.

- The book argues that income inequality has been increasing steadily since the 1980s in the United States and Britain, where high salaries for managers are more acceptable due to changing cultural norms. To combat this, Piketty proposes a global tax on wealth, which he admits is an unlikely policy outcome.

- Piketty says that certain forces, namely the spread of knowledge and skills through education and international trade, are moving in the opposite direction and closing the inequality gap

### Other Ideas

Much of Thomas Piketty's *Capital in the Twenty-First Century* is concerned with how the makeup and ownership of capital* changes over time. But he also examines trends in income.* To explore the issue, he presents data showing what share of a country's total income goes to the different economic layers of the population. He uses data from several countries in Europe, and the United States, as well as less accurate data from some developing countries. He most commonly looks at the income of the richest 10 percent of the population (called the "upper decile,") and the top 1 percent (called the "upper centile").

For Piketty, the richest 1 percent represents a particularly interesting group. It is a small part of the population, but large enough to "exert a significant influence on both the social landscape and the

> **❝** The history of inequality is shaped by the way economic, social, and political actors view what is just and what is not, as well as by the relative power of those actors and the collective choices that result. **❞**
>
> Thomas Piketty, *Capital in the Twenty-First Century*

political and economic order."[1] For example, in the United States, a country of roughly 300 million people, this upper 1 percent consists of three million people whose household income in 2010 exceeded $352,000.[2] This group is much larger than the ruling classes of nineteenth century Europe, which numbered just a few hundred people in each country. It is important to note, however, that thinner slices, such as the top 0.1 percent and top 0.01 percent, also reveal important information about how incomes are distributed in the economy, and Piketty discusses those fractions, as well.

Piketty presents two case studies of inequality, for France and the United States, to show the factors that contribute to changes in how income is spread. In both countries, the share of income taken by the upper 10 percent fell significantly in the early twentieth century and remained low during the period from 1950 to 1980.[3]

In France, the upper decile's share has risen very little since 1980, but the United States has seen a major increase.[4] Although inequality may look similar in both countries, the levels are very different. At times in the early twentieth century, the top 10 percent of earners in France obtained more than 45 percent of total income. In the United States, that group never got more than 25 percent.[5] More recently, the trend has reversed. The upper 10 percent's share in France has remained below 35 percent since 1970. In the United States in the mid-2000s, the upper decile's share reached 50 percent.[6]

## Exploring The Ideas

To Piketty, these changes in income shares are not a "harmonious or spontaneous occurrence"—they are not a smooth and natural trend. Instead, they are shaped by changes in politics, society, and the economy.[7] During the Belle Epoque* at the end of the nineteenth century, and particularly in France, the rich received most of their income from their capital. That led Piketty to describe the period as a "society of *rentiers*"*[8]—people who live off rent they get from their land or income from other types of capital they own. The sharp drop in the income share of the upper 10 percent in France from more than 45 percent in 1914 to less than 30 percent in 1945 was almost entirely due to the destruction of capital caused by "the chaos of war" and the "economic and political shocks" that came along with it.

Wages for the rich did not change much during that period.[9] In fact, interestingly, the makeup of top incomes in France has not changed much over the last eight decades. In 1932, for example, the richest 0.01 percent in France received 60 percent of their income from capital; in 2005, they received just below 60 percent from capital.[10]

Piketty gives a different explanation for the rising income inequality in the United States (and also Britain) since 1980. Unlike the Belle Epoque in France, the recent spike in inequality in America is mainly due to increases in labor income, not capital income, in particular the rapid increase in salaries for managers. "In all the English-speaking countries, the primary reason for increased income inequality in recent decades is the rise of the supermanager in both the financial and non-financial sectors."[11] These "supermanagers" work in many industries and are defined as "top executives of large firms who have managed to obtain extremely high, historically unprecedented compensation packages."[12]

To understand this trend, Piketty draws on sociology as well as economics. Standard economic theory says that wages tend to be set at a worker's marginal productivity*—in other words, at the value of the additional output the company will make by hiring the person. But Piketty finds that, these days, wages of American managers tend to be tied to what society thinks is good, to whom you know, and to the "relative bargaining power of individuals."[13]

Unlike traditional jobs such as grocer or hairdresser, where productivity—how much output they add—can be easily measured, the productivity of managers is nearly impossible to determine. Piketty points out that measuring the marginal productivity of the chief financial officer of a $5-billion company is "clearly impossible."[14] Managers' salaries, then, must be tied to what managers negotiate rather than their marginal product.

This is where society's norms come in. If it is not socially acceptable to receive an annual salary of $5 million, managers will tend to seek lower salaries. But if high salaries are viewed as fair compensation for skill and hard work, then salaries will rise. According to Piketty, "Wage inequalities increased rapidly in the United States and Britain because US and British corporations became much more tolerant of extremely generous pay packages after 1970."[15]

Another secondary idea in *Capital*, laid out in the book's final quarter, is the author's suggestion of a progressive* global tax on capital—an internationally agreed tax on the rich, with the highest taxes for people with the greatest wealth. This would obviously reduce the return on capital, since part of that return would go to the tax collector. In addition, the scheme would also "generate information about the distribution of wealth."[16] Such a tax would give governments "reliable data about the evolution of global wealth," which would also help researchers to better study inequality trends.[17]

## Overlooked

*Capital* focuses on the growing income and wealth gap between rich and poor. Alongside this, Picketty also recognises important forces that are moving in the opposite direction and narrowing the gap.

The strongest of such forces is "the diffusion of knowledge and skills"—in other words, the spread of knowledge of how to better produce or do things, both within and across borders.[18] Piketty notes that the spread of knowledge cannot be expected to happen naturally or spontaneously. Companies, universities, and organizations must promote it. At the domestic level, it "depends in large part on educational policies, access to training and to the acquisition of appropriate skills."[19] At the international level, reduced barriers to trade aid the spread of knowledge. Also helpful is improving access to loans for companies so they can invest in new technologies. When countries trade with each other, they share technological know-how that can then be applied in new ways and spread to new industries.[20]

Piketty challenges other trends that are also often thought to reduce inequality. For example, at the international level, it is widely believed that investments by rich countries in assets in developing countries that give big returns—for example, oil fields or diamond mines—help reduce inequality.[21] The idea is that as capital accumulates in rich countries, it can be more efficiently put to use supporting growth in poor countries that themselves lack capital.

Piketty pushes against this view. He accepts that the injection of capital might be a force to boost production in a poor country, although he adds that this often does not mean increasing income there, since a big part of the income may go to the foreign investors.[22] Furthermore, Piketty notes that countries with a large portion of their industry in the hands of foreign investors have been less successful in promoting growth. That is "because they have tended to specialize in areas without much prospect of future development,"[23] like mining and agriculture, but not in processing or manufacturing higher-value goods.

## NOTES

1    Thomas Piketty, *Capital in the Twenty-First Century* (Cambridge: Harvard University Press, 2014), 254.

2    Piketty, *Capital*, 292.

3    Piketty, *Capital*, 272–292.

4    Piketty, *Capital*, 272–292.

5    Piketty, *Capital*, 272–292.

6    Piketty, *Capital*, 291.

7    Piketty, *Capital*, 271.

8    Piketty, *Capital*, 276.

9    Piketty, *Capital*, 276.

10   Piketty, *Capital*, 276–277.

11   Piketty, *Capital*, 315.

12   Piketty, *Capital*, 302.

13   Piketty, *Capital*, 332.

14   Piketty, *Capital*, 331.

15   Piketty, *Capital*, 332.

16   Piketty, *Capital*, 518.

17   Piketty, *Capital*, 518

18   Piketty, *Capital*, 22.

19   Piketty, *Capital*, 22.

20   Piketty, *Capital*, 71.

21   Piketty, *Capital*, 69.

22   Piketty, *Capital* 70.

23   Piketty, *Capital* 70.

# MODULE 7
## ACHIEVEMENT

## KEY POINTS

- In *Capital in the Twenty-First Century* , Thomas Piketty—with help from his collaborators—compiled the most complete collection of data on income and wealth inequality to date.

- In addition to being in a supportive academic setting, Piketty was greatly helped by computers that made it much easier to store and work with data than it had been in the past.

- In addition to limits on the amount of data available, Piketty did not subject all of his data to statistical techniques that are normally used in economics to test for mistakes. Some readers have criticized his conclusions for this reason.

### Assessing The Argument

Thomas Piketty set out to build as complete a picture as possible of income and wealth inequality. He then used that picture to talk about likely future trends in inequality. Using his own research and that of other scholars, he put together the biggest set of data ever created.

Some critics, such as Chris Giles* of the *Financial Times*, have raised questions about where Piketty obtained his data. But those criticisms have mostly not been related to the work's central success in bringing together nearly all of the available information on economic inequality.[1]

That said, the book does not explain many of the technical, behind-the-scenes aspects of taking data from different sources, cleaning it up, and putting it into a standard form. As a result, some readers may wonder exactly how Piketty reached some of his

> ❝ Piketty has written a truly superb book. It's a work that melds grand historical sweep— when was the last time you heard an economist invoke Jane Austen and Balzac?—with painstaking data analysis. And even though Piketty mocks the economics profession for its "childish passion for economics," underlying his discussion is a tour de force of economic modeling, an approach that integrates the analysis of economic growth with that of the distribution of income and wealth. This is a book that will change both the way we think about society and the way we do economics. ❞
>
> Paul Krugman, "Why We're in a New Gilded Age," *New York Review of Books*

conclusions. To fully understand the way Piketty and his team put all their data together, readers can see the technical appendix published online.[2]

Piketty uses standard economics techniques to interpret his data, although he sometimes does not make that clear. As just one example, when Piketty discusses the capital* stock, he is actually referring to the capital stock after depreciation*—that is, after the loss in value that many assets, such as machines or buildings, often suffer over time. But he does not say that plainly in the text. Most economics journals would require authors to state clearly whether they are talking about capital stock *before* or *after* depreciation.

### Achievement In Context

Piketty wrote *Capital* with all the support and academic freedom a scholar at a university in a western country can expect. He was not bullied or censored when writing the book. As a well-known professor at the Paris School of Economics,* he had access to research grants, university resources, and an audience for his work. France's elite School for Advanced Studies in the Social Sciences* financially supported Piketty, and he partnered with scholars from France, the United States, Sweden, Britain, and China, among other countries.

An important factor in making this work possible was computer technology that could easily process large collections of data. As Piketty notes, as recently as the 1970s, researchers kept data on index cards and so had little time for making sense of it: "In many cases, the technical difficulties absorbed much of their energy, taking precedence over analysis and interpretation."[3]

The methods that Piketty used to analyze his data are not very complex but without the computing tools available to him he could not have produced his book. Piketty used standard computer spreadsheets to analyze and store his data. This allowed him to share his data widely. As the *New York Times* notes: "Because advanced training is not required to examine a spreadsheet, by working in one, and sharing it, Mr. Piketty made it possible for more people to check his work."[4]

## Limitations

Piketty's work, like all works of economic history, depends on how much historical data can be found. Since he based his analysis on tax returns, he has little to say about periods when no taxes were collected. Perhaps more important, Piketty's data focuses on the countries of Europe and North America. Though he tries to study the income patterns of other countries, the data for most of the world has yet to be collected or is not available at all. Piketty put together a larger data collection than what was available to any scholar before. However, it is not complete and if new sources of data are found, they might weaken some of his conclusions, just as Piketty's data undermined the findings of Simon Kuznets* in the 1950s in America.

In addition to weaknesses due to a lack of data, some of Piketty's critics have claimed that he did not follow standard economic methods. In particular, he does not use basic statistical analysis to test his main point: that the level of inequality depends on how the rate of return on capital, $r$, compares to the growth rate of the economy, $g$. As economists Daron Acemoglu* and James Robinson* note, "Piketty does not engage in hypothesis testing, statistical analysis of causation, or even correlation."[5] In a standard economic analysis, economists would test any claim of the type, "A causes B," with these techniques. They could then test if other factors may have influenced the outcomes. In their own statistical tests, Acemoglu and Robinson found only limited evidence that $r > g$ is related to the level of inequality.[6]

Another problem with projects that use huge amounts of data like *Capital* is the challenge of double-checking each entry. Some of Piketty's critics, most notably Chris Giles of the *Financial Times*, have pointed out what seem to be basic spreadsheet errors in Piketty's data.[7] To some extent, such mistakes will always happen when dealing with so much data. But people should keep them in mind when reading the book.

## NOTES

1 Chris Giles, "Piketty Findings Undercut by Errors," *Financial Times*, May 23, 2014, accessed January 15, 2015, http://www.ft.com/intl/cms/s/2/e1f343ca-e281-11e3-89fd-00144feabdc0.html.

2 Thomas Piketty, Capital in the Twenty-First Century (Cambridge: Harvard University Press, 2014) "Technical Appendix."

3 Piketty, *Capital*, 20.

4 "Thomas Piketty and Spreadsheets," The Upshot, *New York Times*, May 26, 2014, accessed February 23, 2015, http://www.nytimes.com/2014/05/26/upshot/how-spreadsheets-can-confuse.html?_r=0&abt=0002&abg=0.

5 Daron Acemoglu and James Robinson, "The Rise and Fall of General Laws of Capitalism," Journal of Economic Perspectives 29 (1): 10, accessed January 20, 2015, http://www.iepecdg.com.br/uploads/artigos/The%20Rise%20and%20Fall%20of%20General%20Laws%20of%20Capitalism.pdf.

6 Acemoglu and Robinson, "Rise and Fall," 14.

# MODULE 8
# PLACE IN THE AUTHOR'S WORK

## KEY POINTS

- Nearly all of Piketty's work has been about questions of income* and wealth* distribution. His earliest work was mostly theoretical, while the work in the 15 years before 2013's *Capital* focused on gathering real-world data.

- *Capital* was the culmination of years of work and several papers on income and wealth inequality. All of these works together explain why Piketty proposes a tax on wealth.

- *Capital* is by far the author's most important work, because it introduced him to a much wider audience and brought all the strands of his earlier work together in a single book.

### Positioning

Thomas Piketty, published *Capital in the Twenty-First Century* at the age of 42, after researching the history of inequality between rich and poor for 15 years. In that sense, it is a mature work and will most likely stand out as Piketty's most important scholarly text.

The author's career is notable for the way he changed direction. In his early years as a scholar, Piketty did mostly theoretical work on how to make public spending more effective. Subsequently, he moved on to a focus that had interested few other economists and seemed a risky way to advance his career: collecting and analyzing data on wealth and income inequality.

Still, Piketty's early work shows a lifelong interest in how resources are distributed in society. A 1995 paper entitled "Social Mobility and Redistributive Politics," for example, presents a "rational-learning theory." It states that what people earn in their careers depends in part

> ❝ Social scientific research is and always will be tentative and imperfect. It does not claim to transform economics, sociology, and history into exact sciences. But by patiently searching for facts and patterns and calmly analyzing the economic, social, and political mechanisms that might explain them, it can help inform debate and focus attention on the right questions. ❞
>
> Thomas Piketty, *Capital in the Twenty-First Century*

on what they grow up expecting, often due to what their parents earned.

Piketty's model also looks at how people vote on candidates or policies that would tax the wealthy to help the poor. He finds that choices can be explained by the "rational" decisions of voters based on their own experiences. If they were born poor, they are more likely to "rationally" believe that policies aimed at giving the poor a hand up are the best way to reduce poverty. If they were born rich, they may more likely "rationally" feel individual effort is the most important thing.

The work of searching out the data that is central for *Capital* began when Piketty returned to Paris from the United States in 1996. In 2001, he published a paper in French titled "Les inégalités dans le long terme" ("Inequalities over the Long-term") that tracked high incomes in France. It attracted the attention of French economist Emmanuel Saez* and British economist Anthony Atkinson.*[1]

Atkinson's interest, in particular, led Piketty to expand this work to cover a much larger geographic area. He published a volume on income patterns in 20 countries in 2007.[2] Piketty also began working with Saez on income trends for the United States, which resulted in their widely cited paper, "Income Inequality in the United States, 1913–1998," published in 2003.[3] Many American economists reviewed this paper and argued that inequality trends are best explained by external shocks—wars, crises, and changing government policy—rather than core features of the economy.[4]

*Capital* also includes Piketty's work with economists Gilles Postel-Vinay and Jean-Laurent Rosenthal on inheritance in France. Piketty's work with Saez and Atkinson had focused on income, but he collected data on estate taxes* with Postel-Vinay and Rosenthal that offered insight into long-term trends in wealth in France. This rich data helped Piketty understand "in a more intimate and vivid way" how wealth and capital* interact.[5]

In particular, the data showed how important the shocks of the early twentieth century—for example the World Wars* and the Great Depression*—were to changing the makeup of wealth in France. Piketty found an important shift had taken place: from real estate as the main form of wealth to "moveable assets," such as money, stocks, and jewels. He also found the average rich person had gotten older.[6]

Piketty's key idea in *Capital* is that, in the long term, inequality is driven by the difference in the return on capital and the growth rate of the economy. This idea also appeared in some of his earlier work. In a highly theoretical 2012 paper, Piketty and Saez developed a mathematical model to identify the ideal rate of taxation on capital. The standard economic model says the ideal rate would be zero. But the authors reconsider common ideas about inheritance and savings and show that a positive tax on capital (a tax rate of more than zero) may be best. Based on their idea that "the average rate of return $r$ on capital is typically much larger than the growth rate $g$," the authors state that inherited capital will tend to grow quickly and "society can become dominated by *rentiers*."*[7] An estate tax would at least slow that trend.

### Integration

Piketty's body of work shows him to be a scholar with a clear interest in the link between markets, the public good, and the proper role of government in society. His theoretical work is not especially important, but it shows Piketty's concern with how wealth is distributed in society.

An example is his 1997 paper, "The Dynamics of the Wealth Distribution and the Interest Rate with Credit Rationing," which shows seeds of some of the ideas that emerge in *Capital*.[8] In his work with the real-world data he has collected, Piketty's most important contribution may be his sheer determination to analyze French inequality. This was in part what brought together the many other scholars who made it possible for *Capital* to look at the issues across a number of countries. Atkinson, for example, says Piketty's research on France "stimulated [him] to put together the material [he] had been collecting for the UK for a number of years."[9]

Most people will grasp Piketty's ideas just by reading *Capital*. But more technically oriented readers may want to read Piketty's earlier work to appreciate the whole process that he went through to arrive at his conclusions. For example, the data in *Capital* is based on statistical estimates that Piketty clearly explains in earlier papers. Knowing these methods is not vital for understanding the book, but they provide some understanding as to why the book is original. Further, readers of Piketty's theoretical paper on capital taxation, written with Saez, will better understand why he has proposed a wealth tax.

### Significance

As the culmination of many years of work, *Capital* is by far Piketty's most important writing to date. Each of his earlier works studied inequality in one country or another, or focused on either income or wealth alone. *Capital* however, looks at the issues together as one whole.

This allows Piketty to make claims that are much more general than he otherwise would be able to do. His discovery that his famous inequality $r > g$ remained true across time and in many countries gives the argument greater power than it would had it only applied to

France or the United States. This makes it easy to forget the geographic and historical limits of the book. *Capital* still deals mostly with Europe and the United States, and depends chiefly on data from France. Further, the book covers as much history as the data allows, but still only deals with the period and places under study. It is possible, for example, that an in-depth analysis of inequality in China would tell a very different story.

Piketty's reputation, and the chance that *Capital* could inspire a new academic school of thought, will depend in part on what graduate students and young scholars think of his critique of the economics profession. Piketty has claimed that in economics "too much energy has been and still is being wasted on pure theoretical speculation."[10] The general shift in economics towards work based on real-world data shows Piketty's view may be taking hold. It remains unclear whether *Capital* will be a central text in future economic thought.

## NOTES

1   Thomas Piketty, *Capital in the Twenty-First Century* (Cambridge: Harvard University Press, 2014), vii.

2   Anthony Atkinson and Thomas Piketty, *Top Incomes over the Twentieth Century: A Contrast between Continental European and English-Speaking Countries* (Oxford: Oxford University Press, 2007).

3   Thomas Piketty and Emmanuel Saez, "Income Inequality in the United States, 1913–1998," Quarterly Journal of Economics 118 (2003): 4.

4   Thomas Piketty and Emmanuel Saez, "Response to Alan Reynolds," *Wall Street Journal*, December 20, 2006, accessed January 19, 2015, http://eml.berkeley.edu/~saez/answer-WSJreynolds.pdf.

5   Piketty, *Capital*, vii.

6   Thomas Piketty, Gilles Postel-Vinay, and Jean-Laurent Rosenthal, "Wealth Concentration in a Developing Economy: Paris and France, 1807–1994," *The American Economic Review* 96 (2006), 236–256.

7   Thomas Piketty and Emmanuel Saez, "A Theory of Optimal Capital Taxation," *NBER Working Paper Series* 17989 (April 2012), 38–39.

8   Thomas Piketty, "The Dynamics of the Wealth Distribution and the Interest
    Rate with Credit Rationing," *The Review of Economic Studies* 64, no. 2
    (1997): 173–189.

9   Anthony Atkinson, "Top Incomes in the United Kingdom over the Twentieth
    Century," *Oxford Discussion Papers In Economic and Social History*,
    accessed February 4, 2015, http://www.nuffield.ox.ac.uk/Economics/
    History/Paper43/43atkinson.pdf.

10  Piketty, *Capital*, 574.

# SECTION 3
## IMPACT

# MODULE 9
# THE FIRST RESPONSES

## KEY POINTS

- Critics of *Capital in the Twenty-First Century* have made specific challenges to Thomas Piketty's data, uncovering some basic errors and claiming that the author overstates some of his conclusions.

- Piketty has responded to criticisms of his data directly, dismissing most of the challenges and clarifying some confusion.

- Some members of the press have said the criticisms of Piketty's book are weak, and there seems to be a trend among economists and even some policy makers to accept some of his ideas.

### Criticism

The English translation of Thomas Piketty's *Capital in the Twenty-First Century* was published in April 2014, six months after the French release. It generated a huge response in the British and American press, both positive and negative. The book received a less excited response in France, in part because Piketty's basic idea that "income inequality is growing and destructive" was already more widely accepted there.[1]

The early criticism of Piketty that gained most attention came from Chris Giles,* the economics editor of a leading British newspaper, the *Financial Times*. In an essay titled, "Data Problems with *Capital in the Twenty-First Century* ," Giles outlines what he sees as several fundamental flaws in Piketty's data. Giles finds an error in importing data from one of Piketty's data sources to the book, leading him to claim, "Frequently, the source material is not the same as the

> 66 The crude seven-word version of Piketty's argument
> is 'rates of return on capital won't diminish.' Is that
> really such a powerful forecast? I say over the next fifty
> or one-hundred years we don't have a very good sense
> of which factors will show diminishing returns and
> which will not. 99
>
> Tyler Cowen, writing in *Marginal Revolution*

numbers [Piketty] publishes."[2]

Giles also finds unexplained changes to Piketty's data. For example, he claims that Piketty "simply adds 2 percentage points" to estimates of the top 1 percent's wealth share in the United States, an error that is "possibly a simple Excel problem,"[3] referring to the widely used computer spread sheet program.

In addition, Giles faults Piketty for relying on simple averages of Britain, France, and Sweden to construct a Europe-wide model of wealth. This, he says, gives incorrect results because the economies are of different sizes. Most important, Giles finds a major difference between Piketty's estimate of wealth inequality in Britain after 1980 and estimates from other sources. Specifically, Piketty's data claims the share of wealth held by the top 10 percent in Britain grew from more than 60 percent in 1980 to roughly 70 percent in 2010;[4] in contrast, Giles's data puts the number at around 50 percent, with little change since 1980.

Clive Crook,* a columnist for the American financial website "Bloomberg View," argues Piketty's data does not support his conclusions. There is a "persistent tension between the limits of the data [Piketty] presents and the grandiosity of the conclusions he draws."[5] Crook claims Piketty's "central contradiction of capitalism"— that the return on capital is greater than the growth rate of the economy, or $r > g$—is in reality only weakly linked to inequality. In order for $r > g$ to drive inequality, Crook argues that the gap between the two must be "sufficiently large" and savings rates must be unusually high.[6]

Further, Crook points out that even during periods when the return on capital was much larger than the growth rate, inequality was high but not increasing. He says this weakens Piketty's claim that inequality will rise in the future. In a commentary in the American magazine *Reason*, economics professor Garret Jones* echoes this criticism. Jones says Piketty does not appreciate the impact of consumption by the wealthy, which "pushes down the growth rate of capital"[7] as the rich spend good parts of their wealth on homes, cars, and luxury goods, instead of investing it.

Former US Treasury* Secretary Lawrence H. Summers,* writing in *Democracy Journal*, also raises the question of consumption by the wealthy. He cites research that finds that "an increase of $1 of wealth leads to an additional $0.05 in spending," or "just enough to offset the accumulation of returns that is central to Piketty."[8] If the wealthy tend to consume more and save less, they will have less to pass on to their children. So Piketty's key ratio of $r > g$ overstates the transfer of capital from generation to generation.

Also, Summers questions Piketty's idea that the return on capital will decline only very slowly as more capital is held by the rich. This point, though technical, is central to Piketty's ideas. Both he and Summers believe that as the amount of capital in the hands of the rich grows bigger, the returns to capital, or the percentage that can be earned by investing it, will fall. However, they disagree about how fast and how far returns will drop.

Technically, the debate centers on the elasticity of substitution*— an economic concept that measures how easily one factor of production can be replaced by another—between capital and labor. Summers says that Piketty's claims about the elasticity of substitution are unrealistic and that future build-up of capital is much more likely to lower the rate of return on capital than Piketty believes.[9] If Summers is right, the rich will grow richer at a slower rate that Piketty expects.

Other early criticisms of Piketty were on philosophical grounds and focused on Piketty's call for a tax on global wealth. The *Economist* magazine praises Piketty's scholarship but claims he "loses credibility" in making proposals for government policy.[10] Similarly, economics professor Tyler Cowen* criticizes Piketty's political positions, saying he "has nothing to say about the practical difficulties, distorting effects, and potential for abuse" that would come from attempting to create a global tax on wealth.[11]

### Responses

Piketty's responses to many of his critics are already included in the text of *Capital* as warnings or conditions to his main argument. For example, expecting Summers's critique, Piketty allows for the possibility that the return on capital may fall a lot, as the stock of capital grows. Although, he claims that typically does not happen "based on historical evolutions observed in Britain and France."[12]

Piketty also responds to the expected criticism that his call for a wealth tax is unworkable. He admits that it is a "utopian idea" that "is hard to imagine the nations of the world agreeing on."[13] Still, he supports the idea as a "worthwhile reference point" to encourage countries to move towards the kind of international cooperation it would require.[14]

Piketty responds directly to criticisms of his data in a letter published in the book's technical appendix. In it, he generally dismisses his critics, writing that he sees the *Financial Times* critique as merely "requests for additional information." He adds that he decided to publish online the whole index, with the huge collection of data he used for the book, to "promote an open and transparent debate."[15]

Piketty admits that his data on wealth inequality is "much less systematic" than his data on income, but rejects the specific criticisms from Giles. For example, Piketty dismisses the survey methods—which "tend to underestimate top wealth shares"—that Giles used to come up with his British data on wealth.[16] In a separate note, Piketty directs Giles to the work of Emmanuel Saez* and Gabriel Zucman, published after *Capital*, which show even greater increases in wealth than Piketty's data.[17]

Piketty also rejects Giles's claim that weighted averages (giving more importance to the data from bigger countries) should have been used to construct his European wealth calculations. Piketty argues that since the form of each country's data was similar, weighting the averages would have made little difference. More generally, Piketty claims his estimates are based on "better methodological choices" than the competing statistics that Giles presented. That said, he accepts that some of the differences between the competing data collections "reflects major uncertainties and limitations in our collective ability to measure recent evolution of wealth inequality."[18]

### Conflict And Consensus

The early conflict between Piketty and the *Financial Times* was never officially settled, as Piketty rejected the criticisms, and the *Financial Times* never changed its position. Some members of the press sided with Piketty, finding Giles's criticisms weak. Neil Irwin in the *New York Times*, for example, accepted that Giles "raised worthwhile issues" about *Capital*, but he added that the "idea that the whole of Mr. Piketty's argument rests on a few shaky assumptions seems unfair."[19] The economist and blogger Simon Wren-Lewis largely dismissed Giles's criticisms, saying the "only issue of substance involves trends in the UK wealth income ratio," a relatively minor part of the text.[20]

To resolve the debate entirely, it will probably take more time to look into other data collections with outcomes different from Piketty's. The opinions of most experts seem to be moving in Piketty's direction. Recent political developments back up this trend. US President Obama's* recent 2015 State of the Union Address* showed that the idea of a tax on wealth is now much more politically possible than it was in the recent past. This shows growing acceptance of Piketty's main claim that inequality is rising and is likely to continue to rise.

The more theoretical disputes surrounding the book, such as the question of diminishing returns* on capital, remain areas of uncertainty. It will take more research as well as watching future trends to see if savings rates and the rate of return on capital are at levels that justify Piketty's conclusions.

## NOTES

1   Tyler Cowen and Veronique de Rugy, "Why Piketty's Book Is a Bigger Deal in America Than in France," *New York Times*, April 30, 2014, accessed December 17, 2014, http://www.nytimes.com/2014/04/30/upshot/why-pikettys-book-is-a-bigger-deal-in-america-than-in-france.html?_r=0.

2   Chris Giles, "Data Problems with Capital in the 21st Century," *Financial Times*, May 23, 2104, accessed December 17, 2014, http://piketty.pse.ens.fr/files/capital21c/en/media/FT23052014c.pdf.

3   Giles, "Data Problems."

4   Thomas Piketty, *Capital in the Twenty-First Century* (Cambridge: Harvard University Press, 2014), 344.

5   Clive Crook, "The Most Important Book Ever Is All Wrong," *Bloomberg View*, April 20, 2014, accessed December 17, 2014, http://www.bloombergview.com/articles/2014-04-20/the-most-important-book-ever-is-all-wrong.

6   Crook, "Most Important."

7   Garett Jones, "Living with Inequality," *Reason*, April 26, 2014, accessed December 17, 2014, http://reason.com/archives/2014/04/26/living-with-inequality.

8   Lawrence H. Summers, "The Inequality Puzzle: Piketty Book Review," *Democracy Journal* 33 (2014), http://larrysummers.com/2014/05/14/piketty-book-review-the-inequality-puzzle/.

9   Summers, "The Inequality Puzzle."

10  "A Modern Marx," *The Economist*, May 3, 2014, accessed December 17, 2014, http://www.economist.com/news/leaders/21601512-thomas-pikettys-blockbuster-book-great-piece-scholarship-poor-guide-policy.

11  Tyler Cowen, "Capital Punishment: Why a Global Tax on Wealth Won't End Inequality,"

12  *Foreign Affairs*, May/June 2014, accessed January 20, 2015, http://wwww.foreignaffairs.com/articles/141218/tyler-cowen/capital-punishment. Piketty, *Capital*, 216.

13  Piketty, *Capital*, 515.

14  Piketty, Capital, 515.

15  Thomas Piketty, "Response to FT," May 28 2014, accessed January 19, 2014, http://piketty.pse.ens.fr/files/capital21c/en/PIketty2014TechnicalAppendixResponsetoFT.pdf, last accessed January 19, 2014.

16  Piketty, "Response to the FT."

17  Emmanuel Saez and Gabriel Zucman, "Wealth Inequality in the United Stated Since 1913: Evidence from Capitalized Income Tax Data," *NBER Working Paper* 20625 (2014).

18  Piketty, "Response."

19  Neil Irwin, "Everything You Need to Know About Thomas Piketty vs. the Financial Times," *New York Times*, May 31, 2014, accessed February 4, 2015 http://www.nytimes.com/2014/05/31/upshot/everything-you-need-to-know-about-thomas-piketty-vs-the-financial-times.html?abt=0002&abg=0.

20  Simon Wren-Lewis, "Mistakes," *Mainly Macro,* May 2014, accessed February 4, 2015, http://mainlymacro.blogspot.com/2014/05/mistakes.html.

# THE EVOLVING DEBATE

## KEY POINTS

- *Capital in the Twenty-First Century* has sparked a serious debate among economists about inequality. Many praise the work, but some point to weaknesses in the book. Other experts, meanwhile, argue that Thomas Piketty's central ideas are wrong on technical grounds.

- *Capital* will likely lead to more work in economics focused on real-world data, and inequality specifically. But it is too early to identify any schools of thought emerging from the text at this point.

- *Capital* has significantly changed the economics profession's attitude towards inequality as a topic of study and has energized research in that area.

### Uses And Problems

Following the initial reaction in the news media to Thomas Piketty's *Capital in the Twenty-First Century*, more scholars began to publish their views on it. Many of them echoed early criticisms but brought their own economic theories and competing data to the debate. For the most part, the academic responses to Piketty did not seek to completely reject his arguments but pointed instead to some of their weaknesses.

One such piece, by Matthew Rognlie, a graduate student in economics, focuses on Piketty's theory of capital accumulation,* the amassing of wealth* from production or investment over time. Rognlie argues, "Most evidence suggests diminishing returns [to capital] powerful enough that further accumulation will cause a

> ❝ The failures of these general laws is related to Marx's emphasis on technology and the productive forces as the engine of history while institutions played a marginal role and the central role of political factors, such as who has political power, how it is constrained and exercised, and how this shapes technology and society, was largely ignored.. ❞
>
> Daron Acemoglu and James Robinson, "The Rise and Fall of General Laws of Capitalism

decline in net capital income." In other words, as the amount of capital grows, so much of it will be competing for investment opportunities that the returns (profits or interest) it can achieve will fall, and eventually its share in the economy will shrink.[1]

Rognlie's argument is quite technical and relies on the idea of the elasticity of substitution* between capital* and labor. In short, the elasticity of substitution measures how hard it is for producers to change their production process to use more capital and less labor—or the other way around—to make their products or services. A high elasticity supports Piketty's argument that growth of the stock of capital will not significantly change returns on capital. A low elasticity means capital growth will reduce returns on capital, weakening the power of Piketty's $r > g$ formula and bringing into question Piketty's claims that the rich will grow richer. Summarizing the literature on what economists have found from real-world data, Rognlie says the values needed to support Piketty's argument are "far outside the range of values that most economists believe empirically plausible."[2] In other words, according to Rognlie, Piketty's claims are wrong.

Another strong response to the book, from economists Daron Acemoglu* and James Robinson,* challenges Piketty's "general laws of capitalism."[3] Comparing *Capital* to the works of Karl Marx,*

Acemoglu and Robinson write: "Marx was ultimately led astray because of his disregard of institutions and politics. The same is true of Piketty."[4] The main point of these two critics is that by reducing the economy to just a few simple mathematical expressions, such as $r > g$, Piketty ignores all the political and economic bodies that actually have a greater effect on inequality.

To illustrate their point, Acemoglu and Robinson provide case studies of Sweden and South Africa. The growth of incomes of the top earners in both countries is roughly similar. But if a scholar were to evaluate the two countries based only on Piketty's analysis, they would miss the very different political and economic history that has shaped inequality in each case. As Acemoglu and Robinson note, to understand inequality in South Africa, the history of the former Apartheid regime—with racial segregation and discrimination—and its labor rules are more relevant than Piketty's laws.[5]

## Schools Of Thought

It is too early to see whether Piketty's book will inspire a new school of thought, though it will surely spur more research into economic inequality. Among economists, reactions to the book have often depended on their starting point of view. Economists already concerned with questions about how wealth is spread have largely supported it. Economists more favorable to a free-market approach have challenged or ignored it. Still, the work has received so much attention that it has attracted many more researchers to the inequality question and the technical issues that Piketty explores in the book.

The book may also play a role in changing the economics profession. Piketty has been critical of how math is used in economics these days. He claims economists use mathematics to "impress those economics departments that are less good at math" and to "look more sophisticated"—not always to get closer to economic truth.[6]

The success of *Capital* may then push some graduate programs in economics to shift away from mathematical training and towards analysis of data of real-world situations. The Paris School of Economics,* which Piketty helped establish and where he teaches, may become a global leader in this effort. Graduate students at the Paris School are currently carrying out a number of projects focusing on real-world problems—an approach that is generally different from the often more-theoretical one pursued by many programs based in the United States.

## In Current Scholarship

Piketty is a well-known and active scholar, and his strongest supporters are his co-authors and partners. Perhaps most important among them is the group of scholars with whom Piketty maintains the World Top Incomes Database (WTID),* including Emmanuel Saez,* Facundo Alvaredo, and Anthony Atkinson.*

Beyond that core group, Piketty's supporters include a large contingent of the economics community. The most important of these followers is Paul Krugman,* who has hailed Piketty's work as a "revolution in our understanding of long-term trends in inequality."[7] Krugman's position as columnist for the *New York Times* gives him a larger audience than most economists can reach—and his support has played a big role in Piketty's success.

Another leading economist to support Piketty is Robert Solow,* whose own work created some of the macroeconomic ideas—those concepts dealing with broad and general aspects of an economy—that Piketty uses in *Capital*. In a wide-ranging review of the book, Solow says Piketty "filled the gaps and then some" in economists' understanding of inequality.[8]

Piketty has received some support from outside the academic world as well. One important example is Bill Gates,* the billionaire founder of Microsoft who has turned to supporting humanitarian causes. Although Gates has made specific criticisms of Piketty as well,

73

he has broadly supported his ideas.[9]

Piketty's concepts have also entered the public debate. For example, in his 2015 State of the Union Address,* US President Barack Obama* called for the closing of "loopholes" that allow the "top 1 percent to avoid paying taxes on their accumulated wealth." That statement at least shows how central Piketty's ideas have become in the public–policy debate—and how perhaps he has become the leading thinker in that debate.[10]

## NOTES

1   Matthew Rognlie, "A Note on Piketty and Diminishing Returns to Capital," June 15, 2014, accessed January 15, 2014, http://www.mit.edu/~mrognlie/piketty_diminishing_returns.pdf.

2   Rognlie, "Note," 8.

3   Daron Acemoglu and James A. Robinson, "The Rise and Fall of General Laws of Capitalism," *Journal of Economic Perspectives*, 29 (1).

4   Acemoglu and Robinson, "Rise and Fall," 1.

5   Acemoglu and Robinson, "Rise and Fall," 11.

6   Matthew Yglesias, "Thomas Piketty Doesn't Hate Capitalism: He just wants to fix it," *Vox*, April 24, 2014, accessed January 20,2015, http://www.vox.com/2014/4/24/5643780/who-is-thomas-piketty.

7   Paul Krugman, "Why We're in a New Gilded Age," *New York Review of Books*, May 8, 2014, accessed March 31, 2015, http://www.nybooks.com/articles/archives/2014/may/08/thomas-piketty-new-gilded-age/.

8   Robert Solow, "Thomas Piketty Is Right," *New Republic*, April 22, 2014, accessed December 17, 2014, http://www.newrepublic.com/article/117429/capital-twenty-first-century-thomas-piketty-reviewed.

9   Bill Gates, "Why Inequality Matters," *Gates Notes*, October 13, 2014, accessed January 12, 2014, http://www.gatesnotes.com/Books/Why-Inequality-Matters-Capital-in-21st-Century-Review.

10  Obama, "State of the Union Address," *Medium,* accessed January 20.

# IMPACT AND INFLUENCE TODAY

## KEY POINTS

- *Capital in the Twenty-First Century* is an important book that has spurred a wider debate about inequality. But many of its core ideas are very controversial in the economics community.

- The book is not openly anti-capitalist*, but contrary to the free market approach, it argues that more wealth* is not always good for the economy and too much inequality may also damage democracy.

- Some economists who are critical of Piketty argue that his concern for inequality is misplaced. They say promoting growth and creating more wealth overall is more important than how wealth is distributed.

### Position

Thomas Piketty's *Capital in the Twenty-First Century* remains an important part of the current debate on economic inequality, both for the public and among scholars. For economists, the book is a focus for new research on the links between the economy, wealth, and income.*
In the public discussion—mainly in the mass media—the book is often a dividing line between the political left and right.

Most economists view *Capital* as a great work of data collection and analysis. Still, some of the main conclusions of the book are controversial. For example, a recent poll, conducted by the University of Chicago Booth School of Business, asked 34 well-respected economists to respond to the following statement: "The most powerful force pushing towards greater wealth inequality in the US

> **❝** A decade ago, during the economic boom and before the financial crisis, the desire to understand why "*r* > *g*" equals more inequality would not have been so intense or widespread. The truth, however, is that economic inequality has been a serious problem for most of the world's population for a long time. These inequalities are nothing new in Latin America and Africa—the regions with the most unequal income distribution. And in many countries with historically high inequality, the main driver of the divisions is not *r* > *g* but rather *c* > *h*, where "*c*" stands for corruption and "*h*" for honesty. **❞**
>
> Moises Naim, "Thomas Piketty and the End of Our Peaceful Coexistence With Inequality," *The Atlantic*

since the 1970s is the gap between the after-tax return on capital and the economic growth rate."[1] In other words, the economists were asked to respond to Piketty's suggestion that $r > g$ has driven wealth inequality in recent decades.

Among the 34 scholars, only one supported the position entirely. David Autor of Massachusetts Institute of Technology (MIT) questioned whether inequality has even risen, saying it is "premature to identify the cause of a non-fact."[2] Many of the scholars, including Judith Chevalier of Yale University and Janet Currie of Princeton University pointed to other causes of inequality such as changes in technology, globalization, and education policies. The economic historian Barry Eichengreen* dismissed Piketty's main idea, when he wrote that he "doesn't find $r - g$ ($r$ minus $g$, in other words: the greater value of $r$ that drives Piketty's argument) a particularly useful summary of anything."[3]

It is important to note Piketty's own position is broader than the question asked in the poll. He has said that recent income inequality is due to many factors, such as rising salaries for managers, and that it is not even mainly due to the return on capital. He does, however, believe that, in the long run, the greater returns on capital compared to the economy's growth rate—$r > g$—is what drives the increase in inequality. Still, the responses at the University of Chicago showed a range of opinions, with some of the economists completely rejecting Piketty's basic ideas and others supporting them.

In public debate, Piketty's name has become linked with concerns about rising inequality. For example, an article in the online political and business magazine *Slate*, "Thomas Piketty Won 2014," says Piketty "changed the [inequality] discussion by focusing specifically on wealth."[4] Before *Capital,* the public debate about inequality focused on income; now the debate is taking place on "Piketty's terms." While this has not led to a large-scale political movement demanding taxes on wealth, it has turned the talk towards wealth. Stephen Marche, a culture writer for the magazine *Esquire*, called the book a must-read: "If you want to understand the world, if you want to compress the mechanics of the forces shaping our time, if you want to know the political choices we face, you must read it."[5]

## Interaction

*Capital* is not a plainly anti-capitalist book, but the logic of its argument challenges some of the stronger beliefs of libertarian* free-market supporters. One of Piketty's central themes is that capitalism is not self-correcting when it comes to inequality. He claims that, contrary to many people's beliefs, a market economy does not naturally move towards greater equality. Further, Piketty raises concerns that the extremely high levels of inequality that may come will damage democracy. Also, contrary to the free-market position, the book challenges the view that wealth creation is always good for the economy.

Liberal think tanks (research institutes) and the news media have supported Piketty's position. Writing in *The American Prospect*, a left-leaning magazine, four economists and political scientists hailed the book as a "magnum opus"—a great work—and endorsed Piketty's call for a global wealth tax.[6] The Center for American Progress,* an influential think tank, hosted a talk by Piketty that helped to boost the issue of inequality in the American political debate.[7] In Britain, another think tank, the Fabian Society,* also used the book to bring the inequality discussion to a wider audience, writing that it gives "intellectual ballast to the social democratic case for the reform of capitalism" and exposes "big holes" in accepted economic ideas.[8]

## The Continuing Debate

One of the most important critics of the calls for changes to the capitalist system is the American economist Greg Mankiw.* He argues that Piketty makes the problem of inequality bigger than it really is. He also says that inherited wealth can actually be good for the economy, so he opposes a tax on capital that would reduce what can be passed on to one's children.

Mankiw offers three reasons why families may want to pass wealth on to future generations. First, since "parents care about their children," the desire to provide for future generations is natural. Second, since consumers face "diminishing marginal utility"* (the first mansion you buy will give you more pleasure than the 10th), it is in the best interest of the very wealthy to pass some of their consumption on to future generations, a practice called "consumption smoothing."* Finally, if one generation is very successful, the principle of regression to the mean*—the idea that values tend towards their average over time— would suggest future generations will be less successful. Families therefore will want to provide for future generations because they probably will not be able to earn similar incomes.[9]

Mankiw's premise is that since rich families share wealth across generations for these valid reasons and, at the same time, boost the whole economy, "inherited wealth is not an economic threat." Another leading economist, Deirdre McCloskey,* argues Piketty's concern about inequality is wrong because the question of how well wealth is distributed is less important than the question of how to grow total wealth in the economy. According to McCloskey, market economies have "enormously enriched a humanity now seven times larger than the population in 1800."[10] To McCloskey, the most important question is how to support the kind of advances that made this rich economy possible—in other words, to make sure that the economy still rewards people for taking the risks needed to make huge amounts of wealth.

The position of Mankiw, McCloskey, and several other like-minded economists can be summed up by the phrase, "A rising tide lifts all boats." This phrase was originally credited to American President John F. Kennedy,* although in a different context. It suggests that as the economy grows richer, the poorest are made better off, even if the rich become richer at a faster rate.[11] Another popular image used to describe this idea is that of a pie. Even if the share of the pie taken by the rich is growing, if the total size of the pie is expanding faster, then everybody benefits.

## NOTES

1    "University of Chicago IGM Forum, Piketty on Inequality," accessed January 20, 2015, http://www.igmchicago.org/igm-economic-experts-panel/poll-results?Surv eyID=SV_5v7Rxbk8Z3k3F2t.

2    University of Chicago, "Piketty on Inequality."

3    University of Chicago, "Piketty on Inequality."

4    Jordan Weissmann, "Thomas Piketty Won 2014," *Slate*, December 29, 2014, accessed December 29, 2014, http://www.slate.com/articles/business/moneybox/2014/12/thomas_piketty_s_capital_how_the_french_professor_changed_economics_conversation.html.

5    Stephen Marche, "The Most Important Book of the Twenty-First Century," *Esquire* , accessed January 20, 2015, http://www.esquire.com/blogs/news/thomas-piketty-capital.

6    Jacob Hacker, Paul Pierson, Heather Boushey, and Branko Milanovic, "Piketty's Triumph," *The American Prospect*, March 10, 2014, accessed January 20, 2015, http://prospect.org/article/piketty%E2%80%99s-triumph.

7    "Thomas Piketty presents Capital in the Twenty-First Century," accessed January 20, 2015, https://www.americanprogress.org/events/2014/03/28/86645/thomas-piketty-on-wealth-income-and-inequality/.

8    Stewart Lansley, "Our Essential Books of 2014: *Capital in the Twenty-First Century* by Thomas Piketty," *Fabian Society Book Reviews*, December 22, 2014, accessed December 22, 2014, http://www.fabians.org.uk/our-essential-political-books-of-2014-capital-in-the-twenty-first-century-by-thomas-piketty/.

9    Gregory Mankiw, "How Inherited Wealth Helps the Economy," *New York Times*, June 22, 2014, access January 20, 2015, http://www.nytimes.com/2014/06/22/upshot/how-inherited-wealth-helps-the-economy.html.

10   Deirdre McCloskey, "Measured, unmeasured, mismeasured, and unjustified pessimism: a review essay of Thomas Piketty's *Capital in the Twenty-First Century.*" *Erasmus* 7, no. 2 (2014).

11   American Presidency Project, "Remarks of Senator John F. Kennedy, Municipal Auditorium, Canton Ohio, September 27, 1960," accessed January 20, 2014, http://www.presidency.ucsb.edu/ws/?pid=74231.

# WHERE NEXT?

## KEY POINTS

- In the long term, *Capital in the Twenty-First Century 's* impact will depend on whether its predictions of a widening wealth* gap turn out to be true.

- The book has stimulated a growing trend: economists are increasingly studying real-world, or empirical, situations.

- Published at a good time to gain attention—just after the big financial crisis of 2007–08*—the book has shifted the focus of economists towards income* inequality. It will also have an effect on policy, even if most governments will not go as far as supporting Thomas Piketty's call for a global wealth tax.

### Potential

Positioned as a book about the future, Thomas Piketty's *Capital in the Twenty-First Century* will continue to have an influence, both on the study of inequality and the politics of how wealth is distributed. In part, the book's impact will depend on whether Piketty's most negative expectations about the future come true. If they do, the book will be seen as having well understood the trends, and many of the present-day problems some people have with the book will be forgotten. If, in contrast, inequality does not increase and economic growth is greater than expected, Piketty's critics will probably claim victory.

Where the debate on inequality goes will depend on the focus of the many research projects that the book will surely inspire. Despite the rich and broad analysis *Capital* provides, a number of important questions remain. One area for further research is consumption and

> ❝ The debate over wealth and inequality has generated a lot of partisan heat. I don't have a magic solution for that. But I do know that, even with its flaws, Piketty's work contributes at least as much light as heat. And now I'm eager to see research that brings more light to this important topic. ❞
>
> Bill Gates, "Why Inequality Matters," *Gates Notes*

spending. Piketty briefly mentions the spending patterns of the rich. A more thorough understanding of how consumption patterns change with increases in wealth is needed, but it will require more work.

As for government policy to deal with inequality, this will depend on how acceptable some of Piketty's ideas are in Europe and the United States at a political level. His most radical proposal—a global wealth tax—will surely remain only a goal, countries may adopt less extreme plans. It is difficult to point to any major projects of this kind, but some countries are already taking small steps to increase taxes on the very wealthy. For example, Piketty sees recent attempts to crack down on corporate tax dodgers by the Organisation for Economic Co-operation and Development,* a Paris-based group of 34 mostly developed nations, as a step forward. And recent rule changes by Swiss banks—to be more transparent about the accounts they hold—are an opportunity for greater sharing of tax information across countries.[1]

## Future Directions

The great popularity of Piketty's book would have been difficult to predict. Likewise, it is hard to say which economists will carry on Piketty's work, as the next generation's leading scholars are now just graduate students. One person who may do just that is Gabriel Zucman,* one of Piketty's former students. He has already published several papers on wealth and income inequality, including a review of wealth inequality in the United States, written with Emmanuel Saez*.[2]

Another young scholar working in the area of income and opportunity is Raj Chetty. Alongside three other researchers, Chetty directs the Equality of Opportunity Project* at Harvard University. This is a large-scale project to study data on upward mobility*—the movement from generation to generation into higher social and economic strata—in the United States.[3] The project is similar to *Capital* in its research style. The scholars are using rich, original data to study a single important issue. So far, their results have been striking. While social and economic mobility has remained unchanged, it is much lower in the United States than in other developed countries and there are also big differences among different parts of America.

Another scholar looking at real-world situations to study welfare—how well off people are—is Esther Duflo.* As the co-founder of the Abdul Latif Jameel Poverty Action Lab* at Massachusetts Institute of Technology (MIT), Duflo has been setting up randomized experiments* to study poverty around the world. The goal of these experiments is to see if anti-poverty programs—such as small loans to small businesses—have an impact on welfare. Randomized experiments allow researchers to "quantify how large that impact is" in a thorough way.[4]

The creation of new tools for analyzing data, combined with the fame of works like *Capital* that study real-world data, will continue to push economics towards such data-driven research. As the economist Justin Wolfers wrote in 2012: "The tools of economics will continue to evolve and become more empirical. Economic theory will become a tool we use to structure our investigation of the data."[5]

## Summary

In his review of *Capital*, economist and *New York Times* columnist Paul Krugman* concludes with the following judgment: "It's easy to be cynical about the prospects for [a global wealth tax]. But surely Piketty's masterly diagnosis of where we are and where we're heading makes such a thing considerably more likely. So *Capital in the Twenty-First Century* is an extremely important book on all fronts. Piketty has transformed our economic discourse; we'll never talk about wealth and inequality the same way we used to. "

Krugman's judgment is no doubt slanted toward his own point of view. Still, his position reflects the majority opinion of the economics profession on *Capital's* impact. Piketty's book was published at a time in 2013 when the political debate and the economics community were open to a discussion of economic inequality. Coming when it did, *Capital* helped to make inequality the key economic issue of its time, bringing back a tradition of real–world research that had been largely dormant in the profession since Simon Kuznets's* work in the 1950s.

Anyone who reads *Capital* will gain an education in the economic history of the past three centuries and will meet a strong line of reasoning about some of the most important moral and economic questions of the twentieth century. In that way, Thomas Piketty's *Capital in the 21st Century* is that rare book that challenges the reader to look at questions of the past and apply them to the future.

## NOTES

1   Paul Hannon, "Piketty Sticks to Wealth Proposal, Sees Positive Signs," *Wall Street Journal*, December 19, 2014, accessed December 19, 2014, http://blogs.wsj.com/economics/2014/12/19/piketty-sticks-to-wealth-tax-proposal-sees-positive-signs/.

2   Emmanuel Saez and Gabriel Zucman, *Wealth Inequality in the United States Since 1913: Evidence from Capitalized Income Tax Data*, National Bureau of Economic Research, 2014.

3   Raj Chetty, Nathaniel Hendren, Patrick Kline, and Emmanuel Saetz, "The Equality of Opportunity Project," accessed January 20, 2014, http://www.equality-of-opportunity.org/.

4   *Abdul Latif Jameel Poverty Action Lab*, "Methodology Overview," accessed
    January 21, 2015, http://www.povertyactionlab.org/methodology.

5   Ali Wyne, "Empirics and Psychology: Eight of the World's Top Young
    Economists Discuss Where Their Field Is Going," *Big Think*, accessed
    January 21, 2015,  http://bigthink.com/power-games/empirics-and-
    psychology-eight-of-the-worlds-top-young-economists-discuss-where-their-
    field-is-going.

# GLOSSARY

# GLOSSARY OF TERMS

**Abdul Latif Jameel Poverty Action Lab:** a research center based at the Massachusetts Institute of Technology in the United States that focuses on applying randomized trial methods to the study of poverty worldwide.

**American Dream:** a set of ideals associated with the United States that includes upward social mobility, economic security, and the opportunity to live a happy life.

**Belle *Époque*:** a period in European history dating from 1871 to 1914, named for the relative peace and artistic innovation of the period.

**Berlin Wall:** a wall built by communist East Germany that divided East and West Berlin from 1961 to 1989. It was a key symbol of the barrier between communism and democratic capitalism during the Cold War—the state of tension and rivalry between the two camps until the collapse of the communist bloc between 1989 and 1991.

**Business cycle:** A period of boom (growth) followed by a bust (recession) in the economy over a period of several years. These expansions and contractions of the economy tend to waver around the economy's long-term growth trend.

**Capital:** An economic concept, interchangeable with wealth. It refers to a variety of assets, including stocks and bonds, land, tools and machines, or any other item of value that can be bought and sold. Capital sometimes includes human capital such as education or skills, but Piketty excludes human capital from his analysis.

**Capital accumulation:** the amassing of wealth from production or investment over time. Capital accumulation is considered a central aspect of the study of economics and was at the heart of Karl Marx's critique of capitalism.

**Capital–income ratio:** the number of years of national income required to replenish a country's capital stock. For example, if a country's capital stock is 100 units and its annual income is 20 units, the capital–income ratio is five.

**Capitalism:** an economic system in which private individuals or groups with property rights over their goods and services control industry and trade. The forum in which trade takes place is the marketplace.

**Center for American Progress:** a liberal think tank in Washington, DC, with close connections to the Democratic Party of the United States.

**Classical economists:** the first modern school of economic thought built around the ideas of free trade, the division of labor, and the use of markets to distribute goods in society. Some key classical economists include Adam Smith, John Stuart Mill, Thomas Malthus, and David Ricardo.

**Classical tradition in economics:** the first modern school of economic thought, most often associated with Adam Smith, David Ricardo, Thomas Malthus, and John Stuart Mill. The tradition was active from the late eighteenth century to the mid- to late-nineteenth century. Classical economists generally believed markets to be self-regulating.

**Communism:** an economic system in which the means of

production are collectively owned, originally proposed by Karl Marx. Marx envisioned a communist society as having no social classes.

**Consumption smoothing:** an economic concept that describes people's desire to have a stable path of consumption over time. The concept predicts individual consumption patterns will not be changed by short-term income shocks. People will borrow or spend out of their savings to maintain their level of consumption.

**Declaration of the Rights of Man and the Citizen:** a document, passed in 1789 by the French National Constituent Assembly—the revolutionary assembly of the period—which emphasized universal human rights, equality under the law, and the aim of removing unjust social distinctions.

**Depreciation of capital:** the gradual decrease in the value of capital due to physical wear, obsolescence, or other changes in economic variables.

**Depression (economic):** a severe and prolonged downturn in economic output. Technically, depressions are often defined as either a 10-percent decline in national output or any downturn lasting more than two years.

**Diminishing marginal utility:** an economic concept that holds that the utility gained from consuming the first unit of a good will be greater than subsequent units. For example, the first hamburger will tend to make a hungry person happier than the 10th.

**Diminishing returns:** an economic concept that states that when an input to production is increased, holding other inputs constant, the increase in output will gradually diminish.

**Economic determinism:** according to Piketty, the belief that economic variables have a tendency to move in a specific direction.

**Economic growth:** the increase in the market value of the goods and services produced by an economy over time.

**Efficient markets hypothesis:** the idea that stock market prices efficiently incorporate information, which means that investors cannot outperform the market over time.

**Elasticity of substitution:** an economic concept that measures the substitutability of two units of production or how easily one factor of production can be replaced with another.

**Equality of opportunity project:** a research venture among several scholars—including Raj Chetty and Emmanuel Saez—studying the extent of economic mobility predominantly in the United States. So far the project has found that mobility is lower in the United States than in other developed countries.

**Equilibrium level:** when supply offered for sale (for example, acres of land or numbers of pencils) equals the demand (the amount people willing to buy at a given price). If supply goes up, sellers must lower the price to attract more buyers. If demand goes up, the price will rise, as those who most want what is for sale will outbid the others.

**Estate taxes:** a tax on the transfer of the estate—including property and financial assets—of a deceased person.

**The Fabian Society:** a prominent British think tank closely associated with the Labour Party. The society was founded on socialist principles.

**Financial crisis of 2007–08:** an economic crisis that originated in the United States housing market and spread through much of Europe and beyond. It is considered to be the most significant financial crisis since the Great Depression of the 1930s. Major banks and other financial institutions collapsed and economic activity slumped. Huge government bailouts prevented even greater disaster.

**Fiscal policy:** the use of governmental revenue to influence the economy. Examples include spending on social programs, taxation, and the financing of basic public works projects such as highways and bridges.

**French National Centre for Scientific Research:** the largest governmental research organization in France, covering all aspects of the natural and social sciences.

**French Revolution (1789–99):** term used to describe the political upheaval that began in France in 1789 and lasted for a decade, leading to a dramatic period of reform, the proclamation of the French Republic in 1792, and the violence of the Terror.

**Great Depression:** a major global economic crisis lasting from 1930 to the early 1940s, during which worldwide output dropped by 15 percent. The depression originated with the United States stock market crash of 1929 and spread worldwide. Much of macroeconomics is dedicated to understanding how to prevent future depressions of this type.

**Gross Domestic Product (GDP) and Gross National Product (GNP):** GDP, a leading economic indicator, is the market value of all goods and services within a country's borders at a given time. GNP is the market value of goods and services produced by citizens of country in a given period, regardless of location. The output of an American-owned factory in Kenya, for example, would be included in the US GNP, but not the US GDP.

**Income:** an economic concept that measures the sum of wages, salaries, profits, interest payments, and other forms of earnings in a specified time frame.

**Inductive economics:** in economics, the use of induction refers to observing the world empirically and then developing economic ideas that help generalize those observations.

**Institute for New Economic Thinking:** a think tank and research institute formed following the financial crisis of 2007–08 to develop ideas in economics that can support practical solutions for the major challenges of the twenty-first century.

**Interpolation:** a method used to construct new data points from a range of existing data points. The technique used to perform an interpolation typically depends on assumptions about the process generating the original data.

**Keynesian Economics:** a school of thought in economics that holds the view that governmental interventions in the economy, particularly using fiscal policy, can help reduce the effects of economic crises in the short run.

**Kuznets Curve:** a graph describing economist Simon Kuznets's prediction about how inequality will evolve in market economies. Kuznets thought that as economies moved from an agricultural base to urban environments, inequality would increase, but would then decrease as wages rise.

*Le Père Goriot*: an 1835 novel by French writer Honoré de Balzac. It is considered an example of literary realism and a reflection of Paris at that time.

**Libertarianism:** a political philosophy that upholds liberty as its primary goal. An important aspect of libertarianism is economic liberty, or the view that individuals should be allowed to function in markets with few restrictions.

**Marginal product:** an economic concept measuring the change in output resulting from one additional input. For example, the marginal product of labor is the increase in the firm's output when one extra worker is hired.

**Mercantilist:** the economic theory and policy that a nation's economy would be best served by regulating trade with other countries and accumulating assets such as gold. Mercantilism was the dominant economic ideology in Europe in the sixteenth through eighteenth centuries.

**Modern industrial period:** the historical period following the Industrial Revolution of the late eighteenth century, characterized by the use of industrial and chemical manufacturing practices and significant economic growth.

**Occupy Protests:** a global protest movement against social and economic inequality that emerged following the financial crisis of 2007–08. It began as Occupy Wall Street and was aimed at exposing the excesses of the American financial class, but it later expanded worldwide.

**Organisation for Economic Cooperation and Development (OECD):** an international economic organization with the stated aim of fostering trade between its 34 member countries.

**Paris School of Economics:** a conglomeration of French universities founded in 2006 to grant graduate degrees in economics. It has produced a number of prominent economists, including Esther Duflo and Emmanuel Saez.

**Progressive taxation:** a tax regime in which higher earners are taxed at a higher rate.

**Randomized experiments:** a method for identifying the effectiveness of a treatment on a specific group of people. Randomized experiments are considered the most scientifically rigorous method for evaluating treatment effects and are used across a variety of disciplines.

**Real business cycle theory:** a class of economic models based on the idea that fluctuations in the economy are due to real, as opposed to nominal factors. The theory sees market fluctuations as rational responses to external factors, rather than evidence of irrational behavior.

**Regression to the mean:** the statistical phenomenon that values tend toward their average over time. For example, if a professional basketball player averages 20 points per game and scores 40 points in one game, regression to the mean would suggest that in successive games his points total will move closer to 20.

*Rentiers*: a French word to describe people who receive income from the ownership of capital. The word often refers to landowners who live off the rent from their tenants.

**Savings:** the economic term for all income that is not spent. Savings can be invested in financial assets, projects, retirement accounts, or simply held in cash.

**Scarcity:** the economic problem posed by limited resources and unlimited wants. Economists only study scarce resources, as unlimited resources have no inherent economic value.

**School for Advanced Studies in the Social Sciences:** a French research institution that provides research support and training in the social sciences, particularly economics.

**Soviet Union:** a Communist federation dominated by its largest member, Russia, that stretched from Eastern Europe to the Pacific Ocean from 1922 to 1991 when it collapsed. Formally called the Union of Soviet Socialist Republics (USSR), the Soviet Union was considered one of the two world superpowers during the Cold War.

**State of the Union address:** an annual speech given by the president of the United States to the two houses of the US legislature and other invited guests. The speech typically takes place in January or February and lays out the legislative agenda of the administration.

**Supply and demand framework:** a fundamental concept in economics that prices in markets are determined by the interaction of the supply of something (a good) and the demand for it. When supply increases without changes in demand, prices tend to fall. When demand increases without supply changes, prices rise.

**Upward mobility:** an economic concept describing the movement from generation to generation into higher social and economic strata.

**US Treasury:** the department of the US federal government that prints currency, oversees federal finances, and manages the government's accounts and public debt, among other duties.

**Wealth:** an economic concept, interchangeable with capital, that includes all forms of property—including stocks and bonds, land, and machinery—that can be bought and sold.

**World Top Incomes Database (WTID):** a public database of inequality information for more than 20 countries, in some cases dating back to the twentieth century.

**World War I:** a global war from 1914 to 1918 centered in Europe. The war was fought between the Allies (comprised primarily of Britain, France, and the Russian Empire) and the Central Powers (comprised of Germany, Austria-Hungary, the Ottoman Empire, and Bulgaria).

**World War II:** a global conflict between 1939 and 1945 that pitted the Axis Powers of Nazi Germany, Fascist Italy and Imperial Japan against the Allied nations including Britain, the United States, and the Soviet Union, also known as the Union of Soviet Socialist Republics (USSR).

# PEOPLE MENTIONED IN THE TEXT

**Daron Acemoglu (b. 1967)** is a Turkish-American economist whose work has contributed to the historical study of institutions, the role of education and skills in the economy, and political economy.

**Anthony Atkinson (b. 1944)** is a British economist considered one of the pioneers of inequality research, particularly for Britain. The Atkinson index is an inequality measure named after him.

**Jane Austen (1775–1817)** was a British novelist known for novels such as *Sense and Sensibility* and *Pride and Prejudice*, published in 1811 and 1813 respectively. Her books are known for their ironic description of the landed class in Britain.

**Ben Bernanke (b. 1953)** is an American economist and former chairman of the US Federal Reserve. His tenure at the Federal Reserve coincided with the financial crisis of 2007–08.

**Honoré de Balzac (1799–1850)** was a French novelist best known for his collection of stories, *La Comédie humaine*, which documented social life in France following the reign of Napoleon Bonaparte. His books are examples of literary realism.

**Tyler Cowen (b. 1962)** is an American economist best known as the co-author of the popular economics blog *Marginal Revolution*. Cowen writes from a predominantly libertarian perspective and is known for his support of market principles.

**Barry Eichengreen (b. 1952)** is an American economic historian best known for his work on the Great Depression and other financial crises. His book *Golden Fetters* is considered to be one of the defining texts on the causes of the Depression.

**Eugene Fama (b. 1939)** is an American economist affiliated with the University of Chicago known for his contributions to the efficient-markets approach to macroeconomics.

**Bill Gates (b. 1955)** is an American businessmen and philanthropist best known as the co-founder of Microsoft and the Bill and Melinda Gates Foundation, a charity dedicated to healthcare and education worldwide.

**Chris Giles** is a British journalist currently serving as the economics editor of the *Financial Times*, covering international and British economic issues.

**Herbert Hoover (1874–1964)** was the 31st president of the United States (1929–33). Hoover earned a reputation as a humanitarian during and after World War I as he rescued millions of Europeans from starvation.

**Daniel Kahnemen (b. 1934)** is an Israeli-American economist best known for his work on decision-making. In particular, he has studied how biases, cognitive errors, and risk influence individual decisions.

**John F. Kennedy (1917–63)** was the 35th president of the United States (1961–63). He was assassinated during his first term in office.

**John Maynard Keynes (1883–1946)** was a British economist known for his work on business cycles and macroeconomics, and as the intellectual founder of Keynesian economics. He was also actively involved in the creation of the Bretton Woods institutions that helped govern the global economy following World War II.

**Paul Krugman (b. 1953)** is an American economist whose work on international trade earned him a Nobel Prize in 2008. He is also widely known as a commentator on politics and economics for the *New York Times*.

**Simon Kuznets (1901–85)** was a Belarusian-American economist best known for developing the national accounting methods used today and for his work on inequality. He is considered one of the first empirical economists.

**Robert Lampman (b. 1921)** is an American economist who helped pioneer the study of income distribution and poverty. He is possibly best known for his work on US President John F. Kennedy's Council of Economic Advisors, which was central to the poverty policy of the time.

**Robert Lucas (b. 1937)** is an American economist best known for his work on rational expectations, economics, and macroeconomics in general. The economist Gregory Mankiw called him "the most influential macroeconomist of the last quarter of the twentieth century."

**Thomas Malthus (1766–1834)** was a British political economist best known for his population principle, which holds that human population will be limited by the availability of food. The population principle is one of the first models in economic thinking.

**Gregory Mankiw (b. 1958)** is an American macroeconomist known as the author of a popular undergraduate economics textbook, *Principles of Economics*. As a public servant, Mankiw was the chairman of the Council of Economic Advisors from 2003–05 under US President George W. Bush.

**Karl Marx (1818–83)** was a German philosopher whose works *Capital* and *The Communist Manifesto* form the intellectual basis for communism.

**Deirdre McCloskey (b. 1942)** is an American economist whose work has covered the areas of economic history, the rhetoric of economics, and economic methodology. Her books on what she calls "bourgeois values" are seminal historical studies of the emergence of market economies.

**Barack Obama (b. 1961)** is the 44th president of the United States. He is the first African American to hold that position.

**Raghuram Rajan (b. 1963)** is an Indian economist and the current governor of the Reserve Bank of India. His research areas include banking, corporate finance, and economic development.

**David Ricardo (1772–1823)** was a British political economist known for developing the theory of comparative advantage. He is also known for his systematic and reductive approach to economics, which had a major influence on the discipline.

**James Robinson (b. 1960)** is a British political economist whose work, much of it co-authored with Daron Acemoglu, argues that institutions have a primary role in economic development, and that institutions established well in the past can have a long legacy.

**Ariel Rubinstein (b. 1951)** is an Israeli economist working in the areas of game theory, bounded rationality, and bargaining. He has published several books on economic theory, including the popular textbook *A Course in Game Theory*.

**Emmanuel Saez (b. 1972)** is a French economist best known for his work, with Thomas Piketty, documenting income and wealth inequality for the United States and France.

**Adam Smith (1723–90)** was a Scottish philosopher and political economist best known for his works *The Theory of Moral Sentiments* (1759) and *An Enquiry into the Nature and Causes of the Wealth of Nations* (1776). The latter is widely considered the first modern work of economics.

**Robert Solow (b. 1924)** is an American economist known for developing one of the first rigorous models of economic growth, called the Solow Model.

**Lawrence H. Summers (b. 1954)** is an American economist who has held positions as secretary of the US Treasury, president of Harvard College, and head of the National Economic Council. His academic work focuses on macroeconomics and finance.

**Richard Thaler (b. 1945)** is an American economist best known for his work on behavioral finance, which is the application of psychology and economics to financial markets.

# WORKS CITED

# WORKS CITED

Abdul Latif Jameel Poverty Action Lab. "Methodology Overview." Accessed January 21, 2015.
http://www.povertyactionlab.org/methodology

Acemoglu, Daron and James A. Robinson. "The Rise and Fall of General Laws of Capitalism," *Journal of Economic Perspectives* 29 (1).

American Presidency Project. "Remarks of Senator John F. Kennedy, Municipal Auditorium, Canton Ohio, September 27, 1960." Accessed January 20, 2014.
http://www.presidency.ucsb.edu/ws/?pid=74231

Atkinson, Anthony. "Top Incomes in the United Kingdom over the Twentieth Century." Oxford Discussion Papers in Economic and Social History. Accessed February 4, 2015.
http://www.nuffield.ox.ac.uk/Economics/History/Paper43/43atkinson.pdf

Atkinson, Anthony, and Thomas Piketty. *Top Incomes over the Twentieth Century: A Contrast Between Continental European and English-Speaking Countries.* Oxford: Oxford University Press, 2007.

Atkinson, Anthony, Thomas Piketty, and Emmanuel Saez. "Top Incomes in the Long Run of History." *Journal of Economic Literature* 49, no. 1 (2011): 3–71.

Bureau of Economic Analysis. "GDP: One of the Great Inventions of the 20th Century." Accessed December 17, 2014.
https://www.bea.gov/scb/account_articles/general/0100od/maintext.htm

Camerer, Colin, and Ernst Fehr. "When does 'economic man' dominate social behavior?" *Science* 311, no. 5757 (2006): 47–52.

Cassidy, John. "Forces of Divergence." *New Yorker*, March 31, 2014. Accessed December 1, 2014.
http://www.newyorker.com/magazine/2014/03/31/forces-of-divergence

Chetty, Raj, Nathaniel Hendren, Patrick Kline, and Emmanuel Saetz. "The Equality of Opportunity Project." Accessed January 20, 2014.
http://www.equality-of-opportunity.org/

Cowen, Tyler. "Capital Punishment: Why a Global Tax on Wealth Won't End Inequality." *Foreign Affairs*, May/June 2014. Accessed January 20, 2015.
http://www.foreignaffairs.com/articles/141218/tyler-cowen/capital-punishment

Cowen, Tyler and Veronique de Rugy. "Why Piketty's Book Is a Bigger Deal in America Than in France." *New York Times*, April 30, 2014. Accessed December 17, 2014.

http://www.nytimes.com/2014/04/30/upshot/why-pikettys-book-is-a-bigger-deal-in-america-than-in-france.html?_r=0

Crook, Clive. "The Most Important Book Ever Is All Wrong." *Bloomberg View*, April 20, 2014. Accessed December 17, 2014.
http://www.bloombergview.com/articles/2014-04-20/the-most-important-book-ever-is-all-wrong

# THE MACAT LIBRARY
# BY DISCIPLINE

The Macat Library By Discipline

## AFRICANA STUDIES

Chinua Achebe's *An Image of Africa: Racism in Conrad's Heart of Darkness*
W. E. B. Du Bois's *The Souls of Black Folk*
Zora Neale Huston's *Characteristics of Negro Expression*
Martin Luther King Jr's *Why We Can't Wait*
Toni Morrison's *Playing in the Dark: Whiteness in the American Literary Imagination*

## ANTHROPOLOGY

Arjun Appadurai's *Modernity at Large: Cultural Dimensions of Globalisation*
Philippe Aries's *Centuries of Childhood*
Franz Boas's *Race, Language and Culture*
Kim Chan & Renée Mauborgne's *Blue Ocean Strategy*
Jared Diamond's *Guns, Germs & Steel: the Fate of Human Societies*
Jared Diamond's *Collapse: How Societies Choose to Fail or Survive*
E. E. Evans-Pritchard's *Witchcraft, Oracles and Magic Among the Azande*
James Ferguson's *The Anti-Politics Machine*
Clifford Geertz's *The Interpretation of Cultures*
David Graeber's *Debt: the First 5000 Years*
Karen Ho's *Liquidated: An Ethnography of Wall Street*
Geert Hofstede's *Culture's Consequences: Comparing Values, Behaviors, Institutes and Organizations across Nations*
Claude Levi-Strauss's *Structural Anthropology*
Jay Macleod's *Ain't No Makin' It: Aspirations and Attainment in a Low Income Neighborhood*
Saba Mahmood's *The Politics of Piety: The Islamic Revival and the Feminist Subject*
Marcel Mauss's *The Gift*

## BUSINESS

Jean Lave & Etienne Wenger's *Situated Learning*
Theodore Levitt's *Marketing Myopia*
Burton G. Malkiel's *A Random Walk Down Wall Street*
Douglas McGregor's *The Human Side of Enterprise*
Michael Porter's *Competitive Strategy: Creating and Sustaining Superior Performance*
John Kotter's *Leading Change*
C. K. Prahalad & Gary Hamel's *The Core Competence of the Corporation*

## CRIMINOLOGY

Michelle Alexander's *The New Jim Crow: Mass Incarceration in the Age of Colorblindness*
Michael R Gottfredson & Travis Hirschi's *A General Theory of Crime*
Richard Herrnstein & Charles A. Murray's *The Bell Curve: Intelligence and Class Structure in American Life*
Elizabeth Loftus's *Eyewitness Testimony*
Jay Macleod's *Ain't No Makin' It: Aspirations and Attainment in a Low Income Neighborhood*
Philip Zimbardo's *The Lucifer Effect*

## ECONOMICS

Janet Abu-Lughod's *Before European Hegemony*
Ha-Joon Chang's *Kicking Away the Ladder*
David Brion Davis's *The Problem of Slavery in the Age of Revolution*
Milton Friedman's *The Role of Monetary Policy*
Milton Friedman's *Capitalism and Freedom*
David Graeber's *Debt: the First 5000 Years*
Friedrich Hayek's *The Road to Serfdom*
Karen Ho's *Liquidated: An Ethnography of Wall Street*

John Maynard Keynes's *The General Theory of Employment, Interest and Money*
Charles P. Kindleberger's *Manias, Panics and Crashes*
Robert Lucas's *Why Doesn't Capital Flow from Rich to Poor Countries?*
Burton G. Malkiel's *A Random Walk Down Wall Street*
Thomas Robert Malthus's *An Essay on the Principle of Population*
Karl Marx's *Capital*
Thomas Piketty's *Capital in the Twenty-First Century*
Amartya Sen's *Development as Freedom*
Adam Smith's *The Wealth of Nations*
Nassim Nicholas Taleb's *The Black Swan: The Impact of the Highly Improbable*
Amos Tversky's & Daniel Kahneman's *Judgment under Uncertainty: Heuristics and Biases*
Mahbub Ul Haq's *Reflections on Human Development*
Max Weber's *The Protestant Ethic and the Spirit of Capitalism*

## FEMINISM AND GENDER STUDIES

Judith Butler's *Gender Trouble*
Simone De Beauvoir's *The Second Sex*
Michel Foucault's *History of Sexuality*
Betty Friedan's *The Feminine Mystique*
Saba Mahmood's *The Politics of Piety: The Islamic Revival and the Feminist Subject*
Joan Wallach Scott's *Gender and the Politics of History*
Mary Wollstonecraft's *A Vindication of the Rights of Woman*
Virginia Woolf's *A Room of One's Own*

## GEOGRAPHY

The Brundtland Report's *Our Common Future*
Rachel Carson's *Silent Spring*
Charles Darwin's *On the Origin of Species*
James Ferguson's *The Anti-Politics Machine*
Jane Jacobs's *The Death and Life of Great American Cities*
James Lovelock's *Gaia: A New Look at Life on Earth*
Amartya Sen's *Development as Freedom*
Mathis Wackernagel & William Rees's *Our Ecological Footprint*

## HISTORY

Janet Abu-Lughod's *Before European Hegemony*
Benedict Anderson's *Imagined Communities*
Bernard Bailyn's *The Ideological Origins of the American Revolution*
Hanna Batatu's *The Old Social Classes And The Revolutionary Movements Of Iraq*
Christopher Browning's *Ordinary Men: Reserve Police Batallion 101 and the Final Solution in Poland*
Edmund Burke's *Reflections on the Revolution in France*
William Cronon's *Nature's Metropolis: Chicago And The Great West*
Alfred W. Crosby's *The Columbian Exchange*
Hamid Dabashi's *Iran: A People Interrupted*
David Brion Davis's *The Problem of Slavery in the Age of Revolution*
Nathalie Zemon Davis's *The Return of Martin Guerre*
Jared Diamond's *Guns, Germs & Steel: the Fate of Human Societies*
Frank Dikotter's *Mao's Great Famine*
John W Dower's *War Without Mercy: Race And Power In The Pacific War*
W. E. B. Du Bois's *The Souls of Black Folk*
Richard J. Evans's *In Defence of History*
Lucien Febvre's *The Problem of Unbelief in the 16th Century*
Sheila Fitzpatrick's *Everyday Stalinism*

The Macat Library By Discipline

Eric Foner's *Reconstruction in America*
Michel Foucault's *Discipline and Punish*
Michel Foucault's *History of Sexuality*
Francis Fukuyama's *The End of History and the Last Man*
John Lewis Gaddis's *We Now Know: Rethinking Cold War History*
Ernest Gellner's *Nations and Nationalism*
Eugene Genovese's *Roll, Jordan, Roll: The World the Slaves Made*
Carlo Ginzburg's *The Night Battles*
Daniel Goldhagen's *Hitler's Willing Executioners*
Jack Goldstone's *Revolution and Rebellion in the Early Modern World*
Antonio Gramsci's *The Prison Notebooks*
Alexander Hamilton, John Jay & James Madison's *The Federalist Papers*
Christopher Hill's *The World Turned Upside Down*
Carole Hillenbrand's *The Crusades: Islamic Perspectives*
Thomas Hobbes's *Leviathan*
Eric Hobsbawm's *The Age Of Revolution*
John A. Hobson's *Imperialism: A Study*
Albert Hourani's *History of the Arab Peoples*
Samuel P. Huntington's *The Clash of Civilizations and the Remaking of World Order*
C. L. R. James's *The Black Jacobins*
Tony Judt's *Postwar: A History of Europe Since 1945*
Ernst Kantorowicz's *The King's Two Bodies: A Study in Medieval Political Theology*
Paul Kennedy's *The Rise and Fall of the Great Powers*
Ian Kershaw's *The "Hitler Myth": Image and Reality in the Third Reich*
John Maynard Keynes's *The General Theory of Employment, Interest and Money*
Charles P. Kindleberger's *Manias, Panics and Crashes*
Martin Luther King Jr's *Why We Can't Wait*
Henry Kissinger's *World Order: Reflections on the Character of Nations and the Course of History*
Thomas Kuhn's *The Structure of Scientific Revolutions*
Georges Lefebvre's *The Coming of the French Revolution*
John Locke's *Two Treatises of Government*
Niccolò Machiavelli's *The Prince*
Thomas Robert Malthus's *An Essay on the Principle of Population*
Mahmood Mamdani's *Citizen and Subject: Contemporary Africa And The Legacy Of Late Colonialism*
Karl Marx's *Capital*
Stanley Milgram's *Obedience to Authority*
John Stuart Mill's *On Liberty*
Thomas Paine's *Common Sense*
Thomas Paine's *Rights of Man*
Geoffrey Parker's *Global Crisis: War, Climate Change and Catastrophe in the Seventeenth Century*
Jonathan Riley-Smith's *The First Crusade and the Idea of Crusading*
Jean-Jacques Rousseau's *The Social Contract*
Joan Wallach Scott's *Gender and the Politics of History*
Theda Skocpol's *States and Social Revolutions*
Adam Smith's *The Wealth of Nations*
Timothy Snyder's *Bloodlands: Europe Between Hitler and Stalin*
Sun Tzu's *The Art of War*
Keith Thomas's *Religion and the Decline of Magic*
Thucydides's *The History of the Peloponnesian War*
Frederick Jackson Turner's *The Significance of the Frontier in American History*
Odd Arne Westad's *The Global Cold War: Third World Interventions And The Making Of Our Times*

## LITERATURE

Chinua Achebe's *An Image of Africa: Racism in Conrad's Heart of Darkness*
Roland Barthes's *Mythologies*
Homi K. Bhabha's *The Location of Culture*
Judith Butler's *Gender Trouble*
Simone De Beauvoir's *The Second Sex*
Ferdinand De Saussure's *Course in General Linguistics*
T. S. Eliot's *The Sacred Wood: Essays on Poetry and Criticism*
Zora Neale Huston's *Characteristics of Negro Expression*
Toni Morrison's *Playing in the Dark: Whiteness in the American Literary Imagination*
Edward Said's *Orientalism*
Gayatri Chakravorty Spivak's *Can the Subaltern Speak?*
Mary Wollstonecraft's *A Vindication of the Rights of Women*
Virginia Woolf's *A Room of One's Own*

## PHILOSOPHY

Elizabeth Anscombe's *Modern Moral Philosophy*
Hannah Arendt's *The Human Condition*
Aristotle's *Metaphysics*
Aristotle's *Nicomachean Ethics*
Edmund Gettier's *Is Justified True Belief Knowledge?*
Georg Wilhelm Friedrich Hegel's *Phenomenology of Spirit*
David Hume's *Dialogues Concerning Natural Religion*
David Hume's *The Enquiry for Human Understanding*
Immanuel Kant's *Religion within the Boundaries of Mere Reason*
Immanuel Kant's *Critique of Pure Reason*
Søren Kierkegaard's *The Sickness Unto Death*
Søren Kierkegaard's *Fear and Trembling*
C. S. Lewis's *The Abolition of Man*
Alasdair MacIntyre's *After Virtue*
Marcus Aurelius's *Meditations*
Friedrich Nietzsche's *On the Genealogy of Morality*
Friedrich Nietzsche's *Beyond Good and Evil*
Plato's *Republic*
Plato's *Symposium*
Jean-Jacques Rousseau's *The Social Contract*
Gilbert Ryle's *The Concept of Mind*
Baruch Spinoza's *Ethics*
Sun Tzu's *The Art of War*
Ludwig Wittgenstein's *Philosophical Investigations*

## POLITICS

Benedict Anderson's *Imagined Communities*
Aristotle's *Politics*
Bernard Bailyn's *The Ideological Origins of the American Revolution*
Edmund Burke's *Reflections on the Revolution in France*
John C. Calhoun's *A Disquisition on Government*
Ha-Joon Chang's *Kicking Away the Ladder*
Hamid Dabashi's *Iran: A People Interrupted*
Hamid Dabashi's *Theology of Discontent: The Ideological Foundation of the Islamic Revolution in Iran*
Robert Dahl's *Democracy and its Critics*
Robert Dahl's *Who Governs?*
David Brion Davis's *The Problem of Slavery in the Age of Revolution*

# The Macat Library By Discipline

Alexis De Tocqueville's *Democracy in America*
James Ferguson's *The Anti-Politics Machine*
Frank Dikotter's *Mao's Great Famine*
Sheila Fitzpatrick's *Everyday Stalinism*
Eric Foner's *Reconstruction in America*
Milton Friedman's *Capitalism and Freedom*
Francis Fukuyama's *The End of History and the Last Man*
John Lewis Gaddis's *We Now Know: Rethinking Cold War History*
Ernest Gellner's *Nations and Nationalism*
David Graeber's *Debt: the First 5000 Years*
Antonio Gramsci's *The Prison Notebooks*
Alexander Hamilton, John Jay & James Madison's *The Federalist Papers*
Friedrich Hayek's *The Road to Serfdom*
Christopher Hill's *The World Turned Upside Down*
Thomas Hobbes's *Leviathan*
John A. Hobson's *Imperialism: A Study*
Samuel P. Huntington's *The Clash of Civilizations and the Remaking of World Order*
Tony Judt's *Postwar: A History of Europe Since 1945*
David C. Kang's *China Rising: Peace, Power and Order in East Asia*
Paul Kennedy's *The Rise and Fall of Great Powers*
Robert Keohane's *After Hegemony*
Martin Luther King Jr.'s *Why We Can't Wait*
Henry Kissinger's *World Order: Reflections on the Character of Nations and the Course of History*
John Locke's *Two Treatises of Government*
Niccolò Machiavelli's *The Prince*
Thomas Robert Malthus's *An Essay on the Principle of Population*
Mahmood Mamdani's *Citizen and Subject: Contemporary Africa And The Legacy Of Late Colonialism*
Karl Marx's *Capital*
John Stuart Mill's *On Liberty*
John Stuart Mill's *Utilitarianism*
Hans Morgenthau's *Politics Among Nations*
Thomas Paine's *Common Sense*
Thomas Paine's *Rights of Man*
Thomas Piketty's *Capital in the Twenty-First Century*
Robert D. Putman's *Bowling Alone*
John Rawls's *Theory of Justice*
Jean-Jacques Rousseau's *The Social Contract*
Theda Skocpol's *States and Social Revolutions*
Adam Smith's *The Wealth of Nations*
Sun Tzu's *The Art of War*
Henry David Thoreau's *Civil Disobedience*
Thucydides's *The History of the Peloponnesian War*
Kenneth Waltz's *Theory of International Politics*
Max Weber's *Politics as a Vocation*
Odd Arne Westad's *The Global Cold War: Third World Interventions And The Making Of Our Times*

**POSTCOLONIAL STUDIES**

Roland Barthes's *Mythologies*
Frantz Fanon's *Black Skin, White Masks*
Homi K. Bhabha's *The Location of Culture*
Gustavo Gutierrez's *A Theology of Liberation*
Edward Said's *Orientalism*
Gayatri Chakravorty Spivak's *Can the Subaltern Speak?*

## PSYCHOLOGY

Gordon Allport's *The Nature of Prejudice*
Alan Baddeley & Graham Hitch's *Aggression: A Social Learning Analysis*
Albert Bandura's *Aggression: A Social Learning Analysis*
Leon Festinger's *A Theory of Cognitive Dissonance*
Sigmund Freud's *The Interpretation of Dreams*
Betty Friedan's *The Feminine Mystique*
Michael R. Gottfredson & Travis Hirschi's *A General Theory of Crime*
Eric Hoffer 's *The True Believer: Thoughts on the Nature of Mass Movements*
William James's *Principles of Psychology*
Elizabeth Loftus's *Eyewitness Testimony*
A. H. Maslow's *A Theory of Human Motivation*
Stanley Milgram's *Obedience to Authority*
Steven Pinker's *The Better Angels of Our Nature*
Oliver Sacks's *The Man Who Mistook His Wife For a Hat*
Richard Thaler & Cass Sunstein's *Nudge: Improving Decisions About Health, Wealth and Happiness*
Amos Tversky's *Judgment under Uncertainty: Heuristics and Biases*
Philip Zimbardo's *The Lucifer Effect*

## SCIENCE

Rachel Carson's *Silent Spring*
William Cronon's *Nature's Metropolis: Chicago And The Great West*
Alfred W. Crosby's *The Columbian Exchange*
Charles Darwin's *On the Origin of Species*
Richard Dawkin's *The Selfish Gene*
Thomas Kuhn's *The Structure of Scientific Revolutions*
Geoffrey Parker's *Global Crisis: War, Climate Change and Catastrophe in the Seventeenth Century*
Mathis Wackernagel & William Rees's *Our Ecological Footprint*

## SOCIOLOGY

Michelle Alexander's *The New Jim Crow: Mass Incarceration in the Age of Colorblindness*
Gordon Allport's *The Nature of Prejudice*
Albert Bandura's *Aggression: A Social Learning Analysis*
Hanna Batatu's *The Old Social Classes And The Revolutionary Movements Of Iraq*
Ha-Joon Chang's *Kicking Away the Ladder*
W. E. B. Du Bois's *The Souls of Black Folk*
Émile Durkheim's *On Suicide*
Frantz Fanon's *Black Skin, White Masks*
Frantz Fanon's *The Wretched of the Earth*
Eric Foner's *Reconstruction in America*
Eugene Genovese's *Roll, Jordan, Roll: The World the Slaves Made*
Jack Goldstone's *Revolution and Rebellion in the Early Modern World*
Antonio Gramsci's *The Prison Notebooks*
Richard Herrnstein & Charles A Murray's *The Bell Curve: Intelligence and Class Structure in American Life*
Eric Hoffer 's *The True Believer: Thoughts on the Nature of Mass Movements*
Jane Jacobs's *The Death and Life of Great American Cities*
Robert Lucas's *Why doesn't capital flow from rich to poor countries?*
Jay Macleod's *Ain't No Makin' It: Aspirations and Attainment in a Low Income Neighborhood*
Elaine May's *Homeward Bound: American Families in the Cold War Era*
Douglas McGregor's *The Human Side of Enterprise*
C. Wright Mills's *The Sociological Imagination*

# The Macat Library By Discipline

Thomas Piketty's *Capital in the Twenty-First Century*
Robert D. Putman's *Bowling Alone*
David Riesman's *The Lonely Crowd: A Study of the Changing American Character*
Edward Said's *Orientalism*
Joan Wallach Scott's *Gender and the Politics of History*
Theda Skocpol's *States and Social Revolutions*
Max Weber's *The Protestant Ethic and the Spirit of Capitalism*

## THEOLOGY

Augustine's *Confessions*
Benedict's *Rule of St Benedict*
Gustavo Gutierrez's *A Theology of Liberation*
Carole Hillenbrand's *The Crusades: Islamic Perspectives*
David Hume's *Dialogues Concerning Natural Religion*
Immanuel Kant's *Religion within the Boundaries of Mere Reason*
Ernst Kantorowicz's *The King's Two Bodies: A Study in Medieval Political Theology*
Søren Kierkegaard's *The Sickness Unto Death*
C. S. Lewis's *The Abolition of Man*
Saba Mahmood's *The Politics of Piety: The Islamic Revival and the Feminist Subject*
Baruch Spinoza's *Ethics*
Keith Thomas *Religion and the Decline of Magic*

## COMING SOON

Chris Argyris's *The Individual and the Organisation*
Seyla Benhabib's *The Rights of Others*
Walter Benjamin's *The Work Of Art in the Age of Mechanical Reproduction*
John Berger's *Ways of Seeing*
Pierre Bourdieu's *Outline of a Theory of Practice*
Mary Douglas's *Purity and Danger*
Roland Dworkin's *Taking Rights Seriously*
James G. March's *Exploration and Exploitation in Organisational Learning*
Ikujiro Nonaka's *A Dynamic Theory of Organizational Knowledge Creation*
Griselda Pollock's *Vision and Difference*
Amartya Sen's *Inequality Re-Examined*
Susan Sontag's *On Photography*
Yasser Tabbaa's *The Transformation of Islamic Art*
Ludwig von Mises's *Theory of Money and Credit*

Printed in the United States
by Baker & Taylor Publisher Services